THE ROUTINES OF POLITICS

THE ROUTINES

OF POLITICS

IRA SHARKANSKY
University of Wisconsin

NEW PERSPECTIVES

IN

POLITICAL SCIENCE

VAN NOSTRAND REINHOLD COMPANY
NEW YORK   CINCINNATI   TORONTO
LONDON   MELBOURNE

To

E. E. SCHATTSCHNEIDER,

who started me on the road to political analysis

Van Nostrand Reinhold Company Regional Offices:
Cincinnati   New York   Chicago   Millbrae   Dallas

Van Nostrand Reinhold Company Foreign Offices:
London   Toronto   Melbourne

Published by Van Nostrand Reinhold Company
450 West 33rd Street, New York, N. Y. 10001

Published simultaneously in Canada by
D. Van Nostrand Company (Canada), Ltd.

10 9 8 7 6 5 4 3 2 1

Preface

THIS BOOK WAS BORN AND MATURED AS I WORKED MY WAY through several discrete research projects. The first project centered on the determinants of state government expenditures. During that study, I found myself disagreeing with several respected economists and political scientists who explained state-to-state differences in spending by virtue of differences in the levels of economic resources. They totally neglected the theoretical work of Lindblom and Wildavsky and overlooked a prime set of expenditure determinants, that is, previous levels of expenditure in each state and the practice of budget-makers to advance only incrementally from those levels. I was roundly chided for the simplicity of my finding: "To say that previous expenditures influences current expenditures is not sufficiently interesting or revealing. What influences previous expenditures?"

In defending myself against such queries, I moved closer to the position that many vital decisions about public policy are just as simple as incremental budgeting. Policy-makers are busier than most of us, and they take advantage of many opportunities to make their decisions as simply, i.e., as routinely, as possible. I found that the budget decisions of legislators rely largely on the recommendations of the chief executive, that administrators often look to their neighboring jurisdictions for ideas about a new program rather than seek the ideas of national leaders in their field of policy, and that policy-makers typically ask for more money when they feel a need to improve their programs, often without determining what purchases will bring about the improvements they desire.

The Routines of Politics compiles these observations about the routine nature of much political decision-making. The book's format should make the ideas available to a wide audience. The footnotes refer to a number of more detailed analyses. Chapters 1 and 2 develop the concept of routines and explain how they fit in with other elements of the political process. One feature of routines that I try to follow throughout the book is their conservative nature. By limiting the policy-makers to a few manageable considerations in his decision process, routines help to exclude innovative "inputs" from the policy process. Chapters 3–7 describe several routines that I have gleaned from my own research and that of others. Chapters 8 and 9 describe two prominent institutions that seem devoid of routines—political parties and interest groups. Finally, Chapter 10 returns to the subject of routines and their conservative impact on politics. It shows that routines are not so strong and pervasive that they inflict *rigor mortis* on the political system. Yet it may require a crisis—or a dynamic leader with powerful motivations and political skills—to bring about a significant lapse in the strength of routine decision-rules.

Numerous individuals and organizations have contributed to this volume. My good friends Thomas R. Dye and Richard I. Hofferbert spent many hours listening to some of my early ideas and reading various manuscripts that gradually developed into this book. William G. Andrews read the entire manuscript and made several suggestions that led me to organize the book in a more intelligible fashion and to clarify my central concepts. David Olson read the chapters dealing with electoral behavior, parties and interest groups, and led me to some additional reading and a fuller statement of my thesis. Without the help of these people, the book would not have reached its present stage. Of course, I take full responsibility for the choices made in putting the final package together.

Several institutions provided financial assistance which permitted me to hire research assistance, buy computer time, travel for the sake of interviewing public officials, and take some thinking time away from the classroom. They are the Social Science Research Council's Committee on Governmental and Legal Processes, the Office of General Research at the University of Georgia, the Graduate Research Committee at the University of Wisconsin, and the Center for Policy and Administration at the University of Wisconsin.

At home, my wife, Ina, kept things going, and Stefan and Erica helped to make the whole project worthwhile.

Contents

THE ROUTINES OF POLITICS

I. Grand and Small Explanations of Political Happenings

THIS IS AN EXPLORATION OF CERTAIN ROUTINES IN AMERICAN politics. As the term is used in this book, *routines* are well-defined procedures that precede decisions. There are different types of routines in public affairs. At one level, an electronic computer uses a routine when it decides if a citizen's arithmetic on his tax return is accurate. In a department of public welfare a case-worker employs a routine to determine if a prospective client qualifies for public assistance, and if so, how much. Most routines reflect the working-out by subordinates of policies that have been defined in an explicit manner by their superiors. In this book, however, we develop a special meaning for the concept *routine*. In later chapters, we describe several routines that influence citizens' voting behavior, regulate government expenditures, and shape the ingredients of public services. In this chapter, we discuss the concept of political routines, and analyze its relationship to other concepts that are current in political science. In particular, we relate it to systems theory, and advance the notion that routines tap a dimension of politics that is not well covered in other systems analyses.

A *routine* is a rule used in making decisions that has the following traits: it is employed widely among people who make certain types of decisions; it focuses their attention on a limited number of the considerations that are potentially relevant to their decision, and thereby simplifies decisions that might have been complex; at the same time, it excludes certain considerations from the decisions, and contributes to political stability by making the decisions predictable under most conditions.

Routines lend themselves to *small explanations* in political science. By knowing the routine that precedes a certain type of decision, one can understand some of the conditions under which that type of decision will be made. Because state legislatures generally follow the routine of accepting the governor's

3

budget recommendations, for example, it is possible to understand why some agencies do better than others in the appropriations process: they win the support of the governor. Likewise, because administrators in many government agencies routinely expect that service outputs will increase along with increases in their budgets, it is possible to gain some understanding of their requests for budget increases: they anticipate improvements in their agency's services.

Although an understanding of certain routines provides an immediate comprehension of some policy decisions, the understanding that is achieved will be limited in nature. The routine of relying on the governor's budget cues explains the decisions of state legislators, it does not illuminate the process by which the governor chooses to support some agencies instead of others. And it does not explain *why* the legislators accept the governor's cues. A knowledge of routines will carry the curious intellectual only part of the way toward an understanding of "Why does it work this way?"

Systems theory is one of the *grand explanations* in political science. For the student who is sensitive to its suggestions, systems theory promises guidance toward a complete understanding of important political activity. Systems theory provides a scheme for analyzing relationships between many segments of political, economic, and social processes, and promises to clarify basic phenomena that underlie routine behaviors. Systems theory provides the useful categories of inputs and outputs, and has produced sweeping typologies that label political processes *ascriptive* or *achievement-oriented, particularistic* or *universalistic, diffuse* or *specific.*

The grand sweep of systems theory—as it is often employed—is one characteristic that makes it less than satisfactory. While it attempts to encompass a lot of activity into simple abstractions, it overlooks a number of behaviors that political actors develop in order to facilitate their tasks. These behaviors include routines. The omission of routines from systems theory is unfortunate in three respects. First, routines are important in themselves. They provide small maps of some critical decisions that are made by political actors. Secondly, routines tell us something about the need of political actors to economize on their information. Routines are simplifying devices that officials use to avoid lengthy processes of rational decision-making. It is often "wiser" to employ a routine than to make detailed calculations about the ramifications of alternative decisions for the host of economic, social, and political criteria that are potentially relevant. Thirdly, the use of routines as substitutes for "rational calculations" signals the failure of actors to consider many of the factors that are posited by systems theory. Demands, resources, values, and need-satisfactions are often ignored by decision-makers who focus in myopic fashion upon the procedures required by a particular routine. Before it is possible to comprehend these allegations, however, it will be necessary to outline the major contributions of systems theory to date. Then it will be evident that routines occupy space that is not adequately mapped by systems theory, and imply some strong qualifications about the interactions that are predicted by current systems theory.

THEORIES ABOUT POLITICAL SYSTEMS: ELEMENTS AND EXPECTATIONS

The most elemental concept in systems theory is the interrelationship of parts. The principal message is that political phenomena do not exist in isolation. The behavior of people and institutions reflect the influence of surrounding environments, and their behavior also has implications for other actors. The researcher who is sensitive to systems theory continually asks himself, "What is related to what?" He searches for variables that interact with each other, and his *system* consists of relationships that have particular significance for an understanding of the political process.

Systems do not merely exist. They relate to other systems as recipients or providers of stimuli. The nature of stimuli received and provided helps to define the *functions* of systems. According to one common formulation, the *political system* provides the following functions to other social and economic systems:[1]

1. the authoritative specification of societal goals
2. the mobilization of resources to implement the goals
3. the integration of diverse groups and interests into the society
4. the allocation of advantages and disadvantages to groups and individuals within the society

The unique resource of the political system is its access to the coercive powers of government. Without the capacity of the political system to make and implement authoritative decisions about taxes, services, and regulations, the needs and demands of economic and social systems might flounder in irresolvable controversy.

The political system makes its contributions to society by processing a number of *inputs* received from other systems, and dispensing its contributions (*outputs*) to these systems. *Inputs* include the public's *demands and expectations;* its *resources;* and its *support. Demands and expectations* include peoples' desires for goods and services for their own use (e.g., education, roads, welfare payments, public hospitals); their desire for the regulation of others' behavior (e.g., public safety and health, the enforcement of civil rights guarantees); and their desire for symbolic satisfactions (e.g., patriotic gestures, the celebration of an ethnic or religious heritage). *Resources* include personnel, skills, material, technology, and money. The *support* given to a political system includes the willingness of citizens to pay taxes, to accept the government's regulation of their behavior, patience in the face of adversity, and a willingness to accept the existing political order. The *outputs* produced by a political system take the form of laws, rules, and pronouncements that serve to articulate social goals, provide services, impose regulations, and collect taxes.[2]

The component of the political system that actually produces outputs is the *conversion process.* This includes mechanisms that articulate the demands of interests; aggregate the demands into proposals for public policy; convert proposals into authoritative rules; apply the general rules to specific cases; adjudicate rule conflicts in individual cases; and transmit information about interests, rules, and decisions from mechanism to mechanism within the political system, and between the political system and other systems in society. Mechanisms in the conversion process include the official legislature, administrative agencies, and judiciary, plus the whole range of extra-legal and informal institutions that engage in politics: interest groups, political parties, prominent individuals, and cliques within the legislature or administration.[3]

The concept of *feedback* depicts the influence that earlier outputs of a political system may have upon the demands, resources, and supports that it receives at the present time. Existing tax legislation affects the flow of economic resources into government agencies. Existing public services and regulatory policies influence the satisfactions which citizens feel, and influence the types of demands which they make. Past efforts to foster economic development may affect the social and economic systems in ways that influence both the demands of the population and the resources that are produced by existing tax programs.

The linkage of outputs and inputs that occurs through the process of feedback makes the appearance of a closed system where the decision-makers respond continually to the impact which their own previous decisions have had upon the environment. The diagram used to depict a political system highlights this sense of closure. (See Figure I-1.) The ideal type of political system approaches equilibrium as incumbent decision-makers adjust their outputs to the resources, desires, and supports which they perceive in an effort to minimize dissatisfaction in the environment. However, the equilibrium is not complete. Factors outside the direct control of decision-makers in the political system have an impact on demands, supports, and resources. Moreover, the description of a political system in equilibrium is so abstract as to defy comprehension. The definition of several routines that are found in the conversion process will clarify the tendency of political systems toward equilibrium. We shall argue below that routines occupy space in the conversion process, and add to the predictability, stability, equilibrium, and conservatism that have been cited for the political system.

There is more than one political system that does this work for the economic and social systems. "The political system" is an abstraction made up of many discrete political phenomena, each of which may be conceived as systems in their own right. Each country has its own political system which provides authoritative rules for its citizens; and within countries localized jurisdictions (e.g., the states and communities of the U.S.) have political systems that perform services for their residents. Also, separate institutions at all levels of government may show traits of political systems that exist to serve the needs of their members and other clients. The routines that we consider in this book are best thought of as being used in several political systems. The routine that individuals manifest in their maintenance of

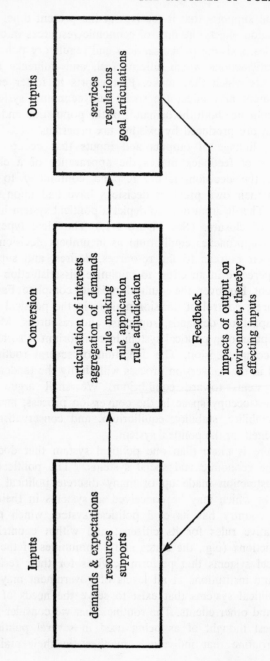

FIGURE I-1
The Political System

Inputs

demands & expectations
resources
supports

Conversion

articulation of interests
aggregation of demands
rule making
rule application
rule adjudication

Outputs

services
regulations
goal articulations

Feedback

impacts of output on
environment, thereby
effecting inputs

stable party identification may be described as part of the electoral system. The routines of incremental budgeting, legislative acceptance of the executive's budget recommendations, and the spending-service cliche appear in the *executive, legislative,* or perhaps the more generally defined *policy-making* systems of the federal, state, and local governments. The routine of regional consultation may be peculiar to systems in state and local governments, although a variant on the basic routine might be found in policy-making systems of federal agencies that administer domestic programs via grants-in-aid to state and local governments; they may adjust their demands on the recipients of the grants according to the region in which the recipient exists.

ROUTINES AND SYSTEMS THEORY

This study of routines should add to our understanding of conversion processes within political systems. Political actors often use routines while they decide what to do in the face of demands, resources, or needs that are presented by their environment. Thus, they use routines to convert inputs into outputs. However, routines also help to isolate the actors from certain inputs. It is in this way that the routines bring equilibrium and conservatism to the political system. Routines that are well-established in the habits of political actors may be used in a similar, rigid fashion despite vast changes in surroundings. Routines may develop in response to certain inputs to a political system, but continue to operate in isolation from other inputs to the system. Richard Fenno has described some decision rules that members of House and Senate Appropriations Committees seem to use routinely in evaluating agency budgets.[4] Because of these routines, it is unlikely that the supporters of individual agencies will obtain a major alteration from standard treatment. One of the questions that is asked in this book is: *Which inputs are ignored by each routine?* Because routines are conservative mechanisms, it is likely they often lead decision-makers to ignore innovative inputs. Or if such inputs come with such power that decision-makers cannot ignore them altogether, routines may blunt their impact on public policy. Yet routines are not altogether inflexible in isolating decision-makers from their environment. On rare occasions individuals ignore their routines and make decisions that are genuinely innovative. Another question that is asked by this book is: *Under what conditions do routines fail?*

The work of Charles Lindblom increases our understanding and provides a theoretical underpinning for routines. In a number of publications,[5] he has described the shortcomings in the decision-making procedure (called *rational comprehensive*) that requires an actor to recognize the full collection of relevant demands, resources, and supports; list all possible policy-alternatives; rank-order his preference for each alternative; define the resources necessary for each alternative; and make policy-choices on the basis of all relevant information. Lindblom sees this approach to decision-making as failing to take account of limitations in the actors' intelligence, time, and policy-discretion. Constraints of time and intelligence restrict their ability to recognize and evaluate all relevant demands, resources, and supports. The constraints of politics and organization limit the announcement of long-range goals and the clear preference-ranking of alternatives. The announcement of goals might arouse conflict among participants who may otherwise agree on a specific course of action. Lindblom's criticism of rational-comprehensive decision-making is a warning against the easy acceptance of systems theory as it is usually explained. Decision-makers seem incapable of considering many of the *inputs* that political scientists have described as influencing public policy. Actors make their choices, according to Lindblom, by means of decision-rules that simplify their alternatives to a few choices and criteria that they may evaluate with relative ease. If such decision rules are used extensively, they become *routines*. Routines are short-cuts which an actor evokes instead of making a full assessment of the system's inputs.

Lindblom has described one decision-process that is among the routines examined in this book: *incrementalism*. It is a routine which is found in many types of government decision-making, but it is found most clearly in the budgetary process. Budget-makers who follow an incremental approach fail to consider all alternatives that face them; they do not rank-preference all the alternatives that face them; and they do not make their decisions on the basis of *all* relevant information. Incrementalists do not debate grand social goals. Their most salient concerns are immediate appropriations for specific agencies rather than long-run benefits for society. They generally accept the legitimacy of established programs and agree to continue the previous level of expenditure. They limit their task by considering only the *increments of change* proposed for the new budget, and by considering the narrow range of goals embodied in the departures from established activities. Their expectations tend to be short-range, pragmatic, and non-ideological.

The principal advantages that Lindblom sees in incrementalism are its compatibility with the limitations of human actors, and the opportunity that it provides for flexibility in the presence of conflicting demands. Incrementalism is particularly suited to a pluralistic society where the debate is not about grand theories of history that Americans strive to reify once and for all time. Most conflict centers around the claims of participants who seek minor changes in established activities. Because increments rather than major changes are at issue, diverse interests can participate in the process without posing major threats to each other. Incremental changes do not commit a program against subsequent modifications and the possibility of satisfying once-disappointed contenders.

Aaron Wildavsky describes several subroutines which actors employ as part of incremental budgeting in the federal government.[6] Agency personnel generally advocate program expansion and budget increases; the Budget Bureau typically cuts agency requests; the House Appropriations Committee routinely cuts agency budgets below the Bureau's recommendations; and the Senate Appropriations Committee acts as a *responsible court* that hears appeals from the decisions of the House Committee and typically increases House grants, but not to the level of the Budget Bureau's recommendation. Like Lindblom, Wildavsky feels it impractical for an actor to consider seriously all the alternatives before him when he considers a budget request. Officials limit their consideration to those values that pertain to the *roles* they choose to play. Wildavsky explains the budget-cutting roles of the Budget Bureau and the House Appropriations Committee as "making sense in the context of agency advocacy."[7] In light of the cutting bias pursued by the Budget

Bureau and the House Appropriations Committee, it also makes
sense for the Senate Appropriations Committee to play the role
of court of appeals. Because agency officials feel they know
most about the needs of their programs and expect reductions
from the Budget Bureau and the House of Representatives, it
makes sense for them to be expansive in their requests.

Thomas J. Anton describes the incremental decision rules
used by participants in the Illinois budget process.[8] Like other
observers of budgeting, Anton finds primary attention given to
an agency's base of existing appropriations and the increment of
new requests. Even more than Wildavsky, however, Anton finds
decision-makers relying on a set of simplistic rules that reveal
little concern for program-related values. Decisions depend almost entirely on the *dollar value* of agency requests as they
compare with *previous budgets* and the *estimates of the revenue*
to be available in the coming biennium. Reviewers cut new
requests without regard to their effect on programs, and administrators in Illinois must often expand services by shifting expenditures from one program to another within budgets that remain
stable in their total funds.

The research of John P. Crecine in the municipalities of
Detroit, Cleveland, and Pittsburgh reveals how budget officers
can make their decisions while remaining oblivious to program
considerations.[9] If total revenues will exceed the sum of existing expenditures, budget-makers allocate the surplus equally
among most agencies on the bases of a fixed set of priorities:
first add to each agency's budget for salaries, then for equipment, and finally for maintenance. If the revenue projection will
require some reductions in the budgets, the same priorities operate in reverse order: reductions are made in most agencies'
budgets for maintenance, and then (if further reductions are
necessary) in equipment, and only finally in salaries.

More clearly than other routines, incremental budgeting reveals its function as a conservative force in the political system.
Budget-makers consider no single criteria so important as their
own decisions of the recent past. Although most government
budgets have moved upward in recent years, the relative position of each unit's budget—among those of comparable units—
has remained stable from one period to the next. Actors in the
system expect incremental change in expenditures: no unit is

likely to show an increase in spending much at odds with the average change, and no unit is likely to suffer the loss of expenditures below the base of the current year. Likewise, the subroutines of incrementalism are predictable. Agency officials expect cuts from the central budget office and the legislature, and perhaps adjust (i.e., pad) their own requests in anticipation. Budget-makers in the central office and the legislature can anticipate an expansionist orientation on the part of the agencies, and adjust their own response accordingly: "Some reduction is necessary to remove the 'fat'."

Incrementalism is not the only routine that is described in this book. It is introduced in this chapter, however, because it is widely described in the literature, and its discussion should clarify the concept of routines. Moreover, incrementalism may be the archetype of routines. There are traces of incremental processes in all the other routines that we examine.

This book does not claim to examine all of the routines in American politics. Basically, it is an exploratory essay whose chief purpose is to point out the routine as a prominent feature of political life, and illustrate this claim with a few examples. The examples come from research in citizens' attitudes, voting behavior, and the policy-making processes of federal, state, and local governments. The resources affected by these routines are enormous. They include most of the expenditures made by American governments, plus the time and skill of public servants that go into the administration of public services. The theoretical significance of routines is impressive. It is helpful to conceive of them within the conversion process (the black box) of political systems. The principal function of a routine for the actors within the conversion process is to simplify complex decisions. Their principal function for social and economic systems is to help maintain inputs and outputs in equilibrium. One of their tantalizing appeals for the policy analyst is their changes in the presence of certain events. When routines fail, it is a sign of significant happenings in the political system.

ROUTINES AND OTHER CONSERVATIVE FORCES

Although routines are prominent among the features that help to stabilize the political system, they are not the only stabilizing factors at work. Other conservative forces include popular values and beliefs that are stable, the persistence of elite groups, and the stability of governmental structures and political institutions. These features should not be confused with routines. Routines are decision rules that are used in an habitual manner by most actors in a given situation. These other stabilizing factors complement the functions that routines serve in the political system. In the next chapter we discuss popular values, beliefs, elites, governmental structures, and political institutions in an effort to place the discussion of routines in the context of other stabilizing forces. We also discuss several varieties of routine, and consider the problem of finding a simple definition for the concept.

ROUTINES TO BE CONSIDERED IN THIS BOOK

Aside from incremental budget-making, we examine the routines inherent in the citizens' maintenance of stable voting allegiances; the legislature's acceptance of the executive's budget-cues; regional consultations of officials seeking new ideas from outside their own jurisdiction; and officials' acceptance of the "spending-service cliche." Each of these routines has in common its ability to simplify complex policy decisions and to bring stability to the political system. However, each routine differs in its form and shape, and in its relationship with other aspects of politics. Moreover, no routine is so inflexible as to preclude change.

We label the routine which stabilizes citizens' party allegiances "like father like son" in order to emphasize the continuity of party ties across generational lines. As in the case of other routines that we shall investigate, the citizen's loyalty to a party label provides him with a device to help make contemporary decisions in the midst of a complex environment. By checking the party affiliations of alternative candidates or issues, an individual employs a simple cue to his own proper assessment of the situation. Party loyalties are persistent in the face of environmental pressures, but they are not rigid. Those occasions when large numbers of individuals abandon—either temporarily or permanently—their habitual loyalties provide us with insights into the events that have profound effect upon the political system.

The legislators' acceptance of the executive's budget-cues are apparent at all three levels of government. We can explain the legislature's reliance on the executive's budget cues by reference to the limited investigatory resources available to legislators. The routine provides one illustration of the way in which officials charged with policy-making duties escape the rigors of making their own independent analysis. By looking at variations in the routine between various state governments, we can evaluate the dependence of the routine on other features of politics and economics. Such features as party competition, the formal powers of the governor, and the amount of slack in governmental resources seem to influence the strength of the routine.

Regional norms and traditions attain permanence through the routine that leads state and local officials to consult with their neighbors when they plan changes in taxes, expenditures, or public services. There is comfort in looking to officials of neighboring states—who often are also friends—rather than to the recognized national leaders in each field of government service. In Chapter IV we discuss regional consultation and its contribution to regional patterns in public policy. The *nationalizing* elements of improved transportation and communication, plus federal grants and regulations have not overwhelmed regional differences in policy. Officials continue to consult with their neighbors, and many new programs that seem to be adopted nationwide show regional variations in their components.

The spending-service cliche asserts that an increase in government expenditures will produce an improvement in public services. This belief appears widespread among public officials, academic political scientists, and economists. It functions as a simplifying routine by relieving decision-makers of the responsibility for making a careful assessment of the factors that actually will improve the quality or quantity of services. In Chapter V we examine the faith in the spending-service cliche, and assess several non-spending factors that may improve services. Although the spending-service cliche simplifies service-planning and political leadership, it is a weak crutch and misdirects many of the investments that American governments make in their programs.

TWO ARENAS WITHOUT ROUTINES

After we describe several routines in politics and policy-making, we consider institutions in which research suggests the absence of important routines: political parties and interest groups. Factors that seem to hinder the development of routines include the large number of people who make important decisions; a lack of systematic training or apprenticeship in which prospective decision-makers may acquire the decision-rules developed by their predecessors; and the fluid nature of an environment in which events are public and highly politicized, and do not accommodate themselves to routine decisions. In most of these traits, parties and interest groups differ from the arenas where we do find routines. The individual voter's routine of party loyalty ("like father like son") benefits from the continuity of an individual's family and personal associations; and the routines of policy-making (incremental budgeting, the legislators' reliance on the executive's budget cue, regional norms, and the spending-service cliche) gain a footing in stable organizations whose members typically have a systematic period of training or apprenticeship before they exercise authority. In the fluid context of parties and interest groups we find certain *principles* that are mentioned by participants and observers. These are decision-rules of a lower order than routines. Principles are not as widely shared by participants, and are not sufficiently clear to prescribe for decision-makers in concrete situations. Many of the principles bear greater resemblance to bland homilies than to rules of decision, and they provide no guidelines as to which of several conflicting principles a decision-maker might employ at the point when he has to make up his mind.

DEVIATIONS AND CHANGES IN ROUTINES

Although routines show—by their nature—considerable isolation and independence from other aspects of politics, their isolation is not complete. Once we accept the importance of routines in politics and policy-making, we can learn about some of the most critical events in politics by examining origins, changes, or deviations in routines. In this book, we do not investigate the beginnings of routines, but we do consider instances when they exhibit marked lapses in effect. We use the lapse in routines as a signal of occasions when basic political relationships are not functioning normally. In a number of cases, we find that changes or deviations in routines reflect other prominent happenings in social, economic, or political events. The coincidence between the lapse in certain routines and major external events provides further demonstration of the central role that routines play in politics. As part of their conservative function, routines protect the political system from frequent upsets. It is only the most critical events, apparently, that can break through a routine, or transform the routines themselves. The list of these critical events includes the depression, war, postwar reconversions, and events that set the legislature against the executive, or elevate the public's regard for certain types of public service.

SUMMARY

Routines are rules that identify for a person how he is supposed to make a certain type of decision. While most routines are employed by subordinates in applying well-ordered administrative directives to specific clients, we focus on routines that have a profound impact on the composition and the policy of governments. The routines of incremental budgeting, the legislature's acceptance of the executive's budget recommendation, and regional consultation guide the decision-maker to rely on certain criteria in making his choices. These criteria, for each routine, are: the previous level of expenditure; the budget recommendation of the chief executive; or the policy-norms which are shared by neighboring jurisdictions in one's region. The routine called the spending-service cliche actually formulates one's decision. When a policy-maker considers the ways in which he can improve his service-output, he is likely to seek an increase in funds without bothering to make a detailed analysis of service needs. When a citizen accepts the routine of party loyalty, he continues his party allegiance from one political campaign to the next; and he relies on the criteria of party affiliation when choosing the side on a political issue or the candidates he will support.

The appeal of all political routines for the decision-maker is their capacity to simplify complex situations. By prescribing a decision, or by identifying those criteria which should be valued highly in making the decision, the routine cuts through the large number of considerations that are potentially relevant for important issues. Routines not only simplify decisions, but they do so in a legitimate manner. They have wide acceptance in the realm of politics. The decisions which they prescribe, or the criteria which they identify as being worthy of consideration are widely recognized and accepted. Routines add to predictability, and reduce the analysis and guesswork that is necessary for the decision-maker.

The concept of routines is useful to the political scientist as well as to the political actor. Routines clarify the operation of the conversion process within the political system. This element—often called the "black box"—transforms the *inputs* of demands, supports, resources, *et al.*, into the *outputs* of decisions that affect taxes, public services, government regulations, and symbolic pronouncements. It is vital for the political theorist to understand that political routines earn their status by simplifying complex situations. They do this by limiting the inputs which are to be considered in making decisions. By doing this, routines isolate the political system from certain inputs. Although no routine appears to be so rigid that it shuts off access to certain inputs, they do make it difficult for current happenings in the social and economic systems to affect decisions. The nature of inputs that are excluded varies among the different routines that we consider. And within the sphere of each routine, the exclusion of certain inputs varies from one period of time to the next. However, all our routines make a conservative contribution to the political system. Where individuals are accustomed to making their decisions according to explicit rules, they tend to resist contrary signs from the environment. Those aspects of politics or policy-making that are highly routinized (e.g. the budgetary process) are likely to reduce the impact which changes in the environment can have on public policy.

NOTES

1. William C. Mitchell, *Sociological Analysis and Politics: The Theories of Talcott Parsons* (Englewood Cliffs: Prentice Hall, 1967), p. 124.

2. H. V. Wiseman, *Political Systems: Some Sociological Approaches* (New York: Frederick A. Praeger, 1966), p. 125.

3. Gabriel A. Almond and G. Bingham Powell, *Comparative Politics: A Development Approach* (Boston: Little-Brown, 1966), Chapter II.

4. Fenno does not write about "routines" *per se,* but he describes certain norms that operate in the appropriations process, and behaviors pursued by the actors in that process that bear great resemblance to our conception of routines. These behaviors include the tendency of the House Appropriations Committee to cut the requests of agencies, and the complementary tendency of the Senate Appropriations Committee to serve as a court of appeals and replace some of the House's cut. Fenno tabulated the budget records of 36 agencies during the 1947–62 period. In 74 percent of the decisions by the House Committee there was a reduction below the request, and in 56 percent of these cases the Senate Committee voted an increase over the House appropriation. The greater uniformity of the House action (i.e., the greater strength of its budget-cutting routine) complements other observations that Fenno makes. The House committee is a more tightly integrated political system, partly because of the clearer demands made upon it by its chamber, and partly because the traditional calendar gives to the House the first, the most prominent, and the lengthiest opportunity for budget review. See his *Power of the Purse: Appropriations Politics in Congress* (Boston: Little-Brown, 1966), especially pp. 353 and 578.

5. See Lindblom's "The Science of Muddling Through," XIX, *Public Administration Review* (Spring 1959), pp. 79–88; "Decision-Making in Taxation and Expenditure," in *Public Finances: Needs, Sources and Utilization,* National Bureau of Economic Research (Princeton: Princeton University Press, 1961), pp. 295–336; and *The Intelligence of Democracy: Decision-Making through Mutual Adjustment* (New York: The Free Press, 1965).

6. Aaron Wildavsky, *The Politics of the Budgetary Process* (Boston: Little, Brown, 1964).

7. *Ibid.,* p. 163.

8. Thomas J. Anton, *The Politics of State Expenditure in Illinois* (Urbana: University of Illinois Press, 1960).

9. John P. Crecine, "A Computer Simulation Model of Municipal Resource Allocation," a paper delivered at the Meeting of the Midwest Conference of Political Science, April 1966.

II. Routines and Other Stabilizers of the Political System

A "ROUTINE" IS A PROCEDURE THAT COMES BEFORE A DECISION. Although there are many types of routines that might be observed, we focus on a few that appear to have importance in the electoral process and in policy-making. We claim much for the concept of routines, but we also are cautious in our claims. Routines are attractive to decision-makers because they simplify complex choices by focusing attention on a few standard criteria. Thus, routines stabilize the political system by limiting the *inputs* that actors are likely to consider in making their decisions, and thereby limiting the degree to which their decisions will range from established practices. Routines also help to stabilize the political system by making certain decisions predictable, and by permitting other actors to anticipate these decisions and to plan their own moves accordingly.

We do not claim that routines are everywhere. Political parties and interest groups are two prominent institutions in American politics that seem to rely on non-routine decision-processes. Although actors in these institutions claim to have certain "principles" of action, these do not have the status of routines. Principles are not widely accepted by participants in parties and interest groups, and they are not precise in the behaviors that they prescribe. *Principles* are closer in their character to the homilies of children's tales than they are to our concept of routines. Like homilies, they are more often expressed than used in making concrete decisions. To the extent that principles can be all things to all people, they are, in effect, nothing of substance to the person who must make a specific decision in the midst of a complex political environment.

In failing to claim that routines can be found widely in the political system, we try to avoid going far beyond the light that is cast by research. Although further inquiry may find additional routines that help to shape the decisions of individual

20

citizens and public officials, it would be dangerous to make such a claim without systematic inquiry. The decision-processes of political actors are often more subtle and circumspect than is evident from initial appearances. What looks like a routine may actually be a screen of simple gestures behind which the actors consider many criteria in an innovative or creative manner. Although we shall suggest other routines that might be verified as such upon investigation, these *suggestions* are not equivalent to the *claims* to be made in Chapters III–VII.

We also avoid the claim that routines are the only—or even the principal—phenomenon that stabilizes the political system. It seems reasonable to claim that political systems—and the American political system perhaps more than many others—has a tendency toward stability and conservatism. We cannot define this tendency with precision, however, and we are not certain of all the features which work in favor of—and against—this conservative tendency. In this chapter we shall identify several other features of American politics which seem likely to complement routines in stabilizing the system. We also offer some hypotheses about interactions between routines and these other stabilizing features, and how they work together to maintain equilibrium in American politics. We also bring together each of the meanings to be assigned to *routines,* and discuss a comprehensive definition of that term.

THE STABILITY OF THE POLITICAL SYSTEM: ROUTINES AND OTHER SOURCES OF CONSERVATISM

Once a writer has sketched the principal features of a political system as inputs, conversion, outputs, and feedback, he will typically posit equilibrium or stability as that state which is achieved as decision-makers (in the conversion process) adjust the outputs of their governmental units to the inputs of expressed needs or demands. The feedback mechanism can help provide an even greater assurance of equilibrium, as the outputs of one moment have an influence over subsequent inputs to the system. The notion of systemic equilibrium that is frequently employed[1] relies heavily on the adjustment of each component in the system to the stimuli received from other components in the system. When these relationships are presented graphically, they provide a neat closure of relationships, and provide a heady feeling of accomplishment to the social scientist as draftsman. However, these abstract relationships do not provide a convincing explanation of equilibrium. Some of the concrete features that are lacking from the explanation are described here.

Several factors that complement routine decision-processes in helping to stabilize American political systems include values and beliefs that have remained strong over periods of several decades; the constancy of elites; structures of government that remain virtually unchanged in their major dimensions; and extragovernmental institutions that operate in much the same way as they did many years ago.

One persistent set of beliefs is a faith in private involvement in government and local control. In the 1830s, Alexis de Tocqueville observed a widespread respect for organizations of citizens that involved themselves in public affairs, and an attachment to local communities as the proper locus of public decision-making. Today as well, public officials consult interested organizations when making policy decisions that affect their members. And most aspirants for public office pay a compliment to local initiative, and state that decisions should be made as close as possible to the people they affect. The country has moved a long way from the time when the national government was decidedly inferior to states and localities as the source of domestic policy decisions. Yet the "drift toward Washington" in policy-making is frequently detoured or slowed by the widely-shared belief that locally governed programs are most desirable. Those who would assign additional responsibilities to the national government show their own awareness of localistic values by the nature of their arguments. It is standard practice to justify an increase in the authority of the national government by stating that local authorities either cannot—or will not—provide the services with their own resources.

Another set of beliefs that persists in American political culture maintains that policy decisions are rational, that voters should approach the polling booth with an assessment of each candidate's proposals in the light of their own best interest, and that the electoral process has a substantial effect on the policies of government.[2] These beliefs persist despite the findings of numerous social scientists that indicate the shortsightedness of such views. Numerous government officials short-circuit rational-comprehensive methods of decision-making, and use such routines as incrementalism and a reliance on the recommendations of other trusted officials. However, the public pronouncements of elected and appointed office-holders give little hint of their real activities. A "full assessment," a "thorough review," the "careful weighing of alternatives" are terms which still dominate the vocabularies of public officials. As part of each campaign for major public office, the contenders and their supporters go through the ritual of preparing and disseminating a program for enactment into policy. They are also likely to accuse their opponents of failing to present a clear or specific platform. Elected officials continue to justify their policy decisions in terms of their mandate from the people, even though it is not feasible to determine from the election results just which aspect of a candidate's appeal led the voters to make decisions in his favor.[3] Such practices may add stability to the system by masking the nature of policy-making, and by detouring the efforts of interest that desire marked changes.

Another stabilizing feature of American political values is the often-described middle-of-the-road nature of political conflict. Many political conflicts find a large number of contenders taking positions relatively close to one another, with relatively few taking positions so far from this center as to present a hindrance to accommodation.[4] The centrist nature of value-conflicts in American politics adds to stability by removing one likely source of severe conflict and revolution: irreconcilable value positions held by large numbers of people. Despite its apparent truthfulness, however, it is possible to exaggerate the notion of middle-of-the-roadism. It applies more to some subcultures within the country than to others, and it overlooks certain value conflicts (such as labor-management disputes in the 1930s and certain aspects of current racial disputes) where large numbers of people take positions that contrast markedly with those of their antagonists. It is also likely that many Americans avoid taking polarized stances on issues not because they accept the centrist position, but because they are oblivious, ignorant, or apathetic about the issue.[5]

A constancy of elites adds stability to American political systems by reinforcing the values and beliefs that are likely to figure strongly in policy-making, and by providing a stability of personnel, background, and training in positions of influence. As in the case of other factors that stabilize the political system, the notion of a persistent elite can be overdrawn. We are not thinking of an elite that is impermeable to outsiders, which is repressive in its treatment of those who aspire to membership, or which is monolithic in its control over all important aspects of policy-making. The composition of elites—in terms of economic, ethnic, and religious characteristics—varies between communities. And within communities, the nature of elites has been found to vary over time, and during one period from one policy arena to another. The elite which influences policy-making in the field of industrial development may be different in membership and outlook from that which is involved in making decisions in education or public welfare.[6] Yet with all these qualifications, several important elites have demonstrated their staying power over time. Their presence may add to the predictability and stability of policy-making within their jurisdiction. In many states and communities of the South, major policy decisions since Reconstruction have been influenced by the low-tax, segregationist values of dominant political groups. In Virginia and Louisiana, state politics have long been dominated by members of the Byrd and Long families, or by office-holders who publicly identified themselves as allies of these clans.[7] In Michigan, a relatively new elite comprised of auto manufacturers and the leaders of the auto workers union have attained prominence in state politics and the affairs of industrial cities. In Massachusetts, several old families have contributed their sons to positions of state and national leadership from the 17th century to the present. And during this century, other elite groups have developed from among politicians of Irish background.[8] For many years, the elite of Tammany Hall governed New York City, while counter elites of liberal Republican reformers sought their removal. In many other states and communities, there are continuities from one campaign—or generation—to the next in the personalities and the positions that are presented to the electorate.

Several features of government structure have remained constant over many years of American history. Among the most important as stabilizers of the political system are federalism, bicameralism, and the committee system in national and state legislatures; a strong seniority system in Congress; single-member districts and simple plurality contests for Congress; and the requirement that the winning presidential candidate receive a majority of votes in the electoral college.

The federal system has remained with us since Independence, and despite the claims of states' rights advocates that the national government has been inflated with unjust powers, the states remain as viable entities in the system. Not only do they enjoy certain constitutional protections, but they benefit from the respect of government officials at all levels, from the state-based nature of American political parties, and from the orientations of states' problems that are necessary among candidates for the national legislature and the Presidency.[9] Political careers are typically born and nurtured in state affairs, and even the most progressive of politicians are loath to challenge the popular value that supports local cultures and the proper role of state (and/or local) officials in sharing policy-making and administration with national agencies. Because the federal system remains viable, we can expect certain variations to persist in public policies. The discussion in Chapter V testifies to the stability of regional patterns in highway, educational, and welfare policies, and in the choice of taxes to be used by state and local governments.[10]

The legislative features of bicameralism, reliance on committees, and a seniority system that are found in many American legislatures[11] together help to isolate policy-making from dramatic innovations. Bicameralism was written into the U.S. Constitution partly to provide then-dominant elites with a check against excessive measures adopted by the popularly elected House of Representatives. It is no longer the Senate which stands as the bulwark against excessive progress. Nonetheless, bicameralism remains as a feature that requires two separate approvals of new programs, and provides the conservative opposition with additional opportunities to stall the innovation. The committee system narrows the arena in which critical decisions will be made on policy. Thus, it stabilizes conflicts by limiting them to a committee arena, and the few interests that are represented there. The seniority system reinforces the conservatism of the committee structure by insuring that committee leaders will be those members with the longest tenure. Insofar as these legislators are also the oldest in age and the least likely to be challenged in their districts by strong opponents, they will be most out of touch with innovative forces in society. Like other features we have mentioned, however, the committee system is not absolute in its influence. The chairmen of some committees have been cited for their efforts on behalf of innovations. Skilled legislative technicians, providing they have the motivation to go all out in support of an issue, may employ procedures that will bypass a committee. The rarity of this procedure in Congress testifies to the support for the committee system in that body.

Since the adoption of the Constitution we have had single member districts and simple plurality contests for the national legislature, and we have required the winning presidential candidate to receive a majority of the electoral college. The constancy of these procedures has stabilized campaign practices by permitting candidates to plan their moves without worry about major changes in the electoral system. These procedures have also hindered the development of viable third parties. The combination of single-member districts and simple plurality contests requires that a fledgling party win a plurality in at least one district to gain representation in the national legislature. Insofar as minor movements tend to falter without the visibility of some members in the national legislature, the lack of a *proportional representation* system probably discourages some candidates from even trying to win outside the context of the major parties. With little hope for success in third parties, virtually all aspiring politicians join one of the established parties. In these parties, innovative policy desires encounter the opposition of established tradition and are likely to be modified accordingly.

The requirement of a majority in the electoral college provides an additional barrier to the formation of third parties, but this works in a different way than the system of single-member districts and simple plurality contests for the legislature. The requirement for an electoral college majority makes it virtually certain that only the candidate of a well-established party having nation-wide strength can capture the presidency. However, the requirement also tempts dissident political factions to make a contest for the presidency in order to deny any candidate an electoral college majority, and thereby a simple presidential victory. So far no third party has used this tactic successfully to gain a firm start in American politics. A few groups have made a serious effort to move outside of the major parties during the last half-century; they failed to make a serious dent in the electoral college or to gain substantial representation in Congress.

The constancy of the Democratic and Republican parties, as well as the stable two-party nature of American politics, provides a measure of stability to American politics. Democrats and Republicans have been the major electoral contenders for over 100 years. They antedate the present form of government in almost all the major countries of the world. Although the issues disputed have changed since John C. Fremont opposed James Buchanan in the presidential election of 1856, the parties have retained familiar policy postures over periods of several decades. It is convenient to date the beginning of the current political era with the depression, and to see a continuity in Democratic and Republican orientations since that time. Although each party has its extreme members and dissident factions that confuse any simple categorization, it is feasible to predict the likely positions of Democratic vs Republican candidates for the presidency on such issues as the scope of domestic programs financed by the national government, and the use of public—as opposed to private—methods for the development of natural resources. Within the political systems of individual states, the nature of conflict distinguishing one party from the other may differ from those issues that have divided each party's contenders for the presidency. But two-party competition is increasing in importance throughout all sections of the country. And where two-party competition is an ingredient in state politics, it is generally possible to discern stable patterns of conflict on key issues.

ROUTINES AND STABILIZING VALUES, ELITES, STRUCTURES AND INSTITUTIONS

Persistent values, elites, structures, and institutions help to stabilize American political systems, but they should be distinguished from routines. Routines are rules that decision-makers follow in making certain kinds of choices. The stable values, elites, structures, and institutions are parts of the background or environment in which routine decisions are made. As elements of the environment, these stable features may encourage decision-makers to employ routines. There is no innovative stimulus apparent in the values, elites, structures, or institutions we have described in this chapter. The persistence of institutional and attitudinal surroundings probably reinforce whatever stabilizing features adhere to routine decision-rules.

At this point our knowledge of routines is primitive. We make no claim to have identified the interactions between routines and the background characteristics of persistent values, elites, structures, and institutions. We know that routines vary in strength, and it seems likely that background elements vary in strength from one situation to another. Both routines and the background features may respond to changes in other features of economic, social, or political systems. By viewing routines and other stabilizing features as variables, we are led to several questions:

1. Under what conditions will political actors use—or depart from—routines in making decisions?

2. In the event that a context suggests the use of different routines, which would be chosen?

3. Which fields of policy-making are most subject to routine decisions, and which are relatively free of routines?

4. What conditions generate the development of new routines?

5. What features of the environment are most important in affecting the individual's decision to use a routine?

6. What situations will permit reformers to modify the routines that actors use?

The routines described in this book probably do not exhaust the list. The discovery of others will increase our ability to describe the political behavior of individuals, policy-making processes, and interactions between routines and other features of the political system that exert a bias in the direction of conservatism. A reading of case studies suggests several additional routines that might profitably be examined. These include:

1. The tendency of regulatory agencies to weigh heavily criteria which protect the interests of the industry that is formally subject to

its regulation. This tendency is claimed in many descriptions of regulatory commissions. It is said to represent the ability of intense, well-organized industry spokesmen to dull the edge of regulatory zeal after do-gooders have left the field of battle, confident that legislation setting up a regulatory body is sufficient to cure past social evils.[12]

2. The tendency of officials charged with enforcement responsibilities to ignore violations that are not severe enough to cause clear harm or inconvenience to many persons. For economic regulations, such a routine might reflect the fear of enforcement officials that powerful elites might be provoked if their actions were subject to inhibiting regulation. In the case of regulations directed against the mass of the population (e.g., traffic laws), such a routine might reflect the officials' concern lest rigid enforcement would lose their agency the support of people who expect the police to exercise flexibility in their judgment.[13]

3. The tendency of people to perceive those stimuli which conform to their prejudice. Selective perception is a familiar concept to social sicentists who investigate communication. It leads people to notice those items in the mass media which reinforce their views about an issue, and to overlook items which challenge their views. Likewise, it leads people to extract from an ambiguous communication those items which confirm their beliefs, and to see these as the essence of the entire communication. Some observers have claimed that President Eisenhower's habit of halting, inarticulate speech containing confusing qualifying phrases served him well. Since the President's audiences were generally pre-disposed in his favor, their use of a selective perception routine may have found for them somewhere in his remarks support for their own views.[14]

A DEFINITION OF ROUTINES

There is no simple definition for the concept of *routines*. As it is used in this book, it has several meanings, although each of them share certain ingredients. They combine features of *procedures, habits,* and *learned behaviors* that are evident in the decision processes of individuals, social groups, and formal organizations. From our vantage point, routines screen inputs to a political system. From another vantage point, routines may appear to be inputs themselves. Some routines merely identify criteria for the decision-maker to consider (e.g., the percentage increment between the current budget and the proposal for next year), while others may specify the decision which an individual should make (e.g., increase spending when an improvement in services is desired). In some contexts, routines are formalized as rules of procedure that officials must follow explicitly in making their decisions, and at other times they evolve implicitly; they may be used by individuals who do not recognize the nature of their decisions, and who might deny the routines which their own decisions reveal. Thus, certain routines may be perceived by observers as well-defined procedures that precede decisions, but be contrary to the decision-maker's own assessment of his activity. Routines also appear inflexible under certain circumstances, but they seem to bend or even disappear under some pressures.

The common features of routines are their appeal to individuals or organizations because they simplify decisions which are potentially complex; their function of permitting some "inputs" to affect conversion processes in a political system while they exclude others; their contribution to political stability by making certain types of decisions predictable—within certain ranges—under most conditions; and their use by most of the decision-makers for whom they are relevant. A decision rule that is developed and used by a limited number of party organizations or interest groups, for example, would not qualify as a routine in our terms because it does not have wide appeal as a device for simplifying decisions, and because it would not make certain types of decisions predictable under most conditions. This also applies to procedures used by some legislatures for selecting new members for their committees, or promoting certain members to committee chairmanships. Notions of interest group balance are used by some congressional committees for selecting their new members, and all congressional committees use seniority rules to select their chairmen. Yet these procedures are not widely used among the state legislatures. In this book we reserve the concept of routines for those decision rules that appear to be followed by a very large number of the individuals or organizations that are engaged in similar activities. In each of the following chapters we argue that specific routines have a wide use.

This book does not claim to be a definitive work on the subject of routines in politics, or even the subject of routines in American politics. It humbly offers the concept of routines as a phenomenon that sheds light on several aspects of politics that have not received sufficient exploration: the conversion processes of political systems. We argue that the routines to be described meet the criteria of simplifying complex decisions; contributing to political stability by making certain types of decisions predictable within certain ranges under most conditions; their exclusion of certain inputs to the conversion process; and their widespread use by most of the decision-makers for whom they are relevant. Although we argue that our routines meet these criteria, we actually lack the technology or the information to say with precision how well each of them meet each criteria. Further research might reveal various classifications of routines that display distinct properties, and have distinct implications for the individuals or organizations who use them. This book focuses more on the common traits of routines than on the features which distinguish one from another. Hopefully, the strength of our arguments will convince most readers to accept the definition of routines as both reasonable and helpful. Yet if some readers should consider the arguments and conclusions unreasonable or premature, it shall be taken as a compliment if they evaluate the basic concepts with improved analytic techniques and/or additional information.

CONCLUSION

In this chapter we have identified several features beside routines which help to stabilize American political systems, and we have suggested several routines beside those to be described extensively in Chapters III-VII. Systems theorists have written casually about the tendency for political systems to maintain equilibrium, reciprocity, or balance between inputs, outputs, and feedback mechanisms. The items discussed in this chapter may "flesh-out" these abstractions.

Although we have noted the contribution of routines and other political factors to stability, it would be misleading to exaggerate this attribute. Political systems do have several ingredients which bias them toward a stable state, but they are not beset with rigor mortis. In Chapter X we list several deviations from each of the principal routines. And in Chapters VII and IX we describe the conditions prevailing in parties and interest groups that discouraged the development of routines. Innovation is a continuing feature in American politics. The examination of stabilizing features is sterile if pursued solely for its own sake. Such an inquiry is not only about, but it may actually be a vital part of the policy-making process. By knowing the source and character of stability in American political systems, we shall be better prepared to reform aspects of the systems that will produce more desirable outputs of public policy.

NOTES

1. H. V. Wiseman, *Political Systems: Some Sociological Approaches* (New York: Frederick A. Praeger, 1966), pp. 114–17.

2. Murray Edelman, *The Symbolic Uses of Politics* (Urbana: University of Illinois Press, 1964), Chapter I.

3. Robert A. Dahl, *A Preface to Democratic Theory* (Chicago: University of Chicago Press, 1956), p. 127 ff.

4. Anthony Downs, *An Economic Theory of Democracy* (New York: Harper and Brothers, 1957), Chapter 8.

5. See E. E. Schattschneider, *The Semi-Sovereign People* (New York: Holt, Rinehart and Winston, 1960).

6. See Robert A. Dahl, *Who Governs?* (New Haven: Yale University Press, 1961).

7. The public-welfare oriented Long clan should not be equated with the economic conservative Byrds. Indeed, their juxtaposition in this context highlights the differences in policy orientations which can distinguish among persistent elites in two states that are equated in the public's mind as equally "southern."

8. The differences in policy-orientation toward foreign affairs shown by grandfather and grandson Lodge testify to the changes in policy attachments that elites may experience over time.

9. See Morton Grodzins, "American Political Parties and the American System," *Western Political Quarterly*, XIII (December 1960), pp. 974–98.

10. For a discussion of regional differences in state politics, see my *Regionalism in American Politics* (Indianapolis: Bobbs-Merrill, 1969).

11. In contrast to the situation in the U.S. Congress, a number of state legislatures fail to employ a senority system in staffing their committees or naming committee chairmen.

12. Edelman, *op.cit.*, Chapter 2.

13. *Ibid*, pp. 44–45.

14. *Ibid, p.* 81.

III. Stable Political Allegiances: Like Father Like Son

THIS CHAPTER BEGINS THE DESCRIPTION OF ROUTINES. ITS FOCUS is the elemental actor in politics: the individual citizen. The routines at issue are those which he employs to simplify his environment and to reach decisions about political issues and the candidates who will receive his vote.

It may appear incongruous to move directly from a theoretical discussion of routines in political systems to a report about the votes and attitudes of individual citizens. There is a sharp change from the macro- to the microscopic. Yet it is proper—and even helpful—to begin a consideration of routines with the individual. In later chapters the discussion will concern the routines followed by complex organizations, but in each case they will be—at heart—the routines that individual participants employ to simplify and manage their environment. The difference between this chapter and later ones is that the routines considered here are employed by individuals for the sake of personal decisions. The routines considered later are developed and used by individuals as part of their jobs in government.

This chapter considers individual citizens not only as *persons,* but as participants in an electoral system. The aggregate of their personal decisions stands as the electorate's choice between competing candidates. To the extent that citizens use conservative routines that tend to perpetuate their own past voting habits, these routines make a stabilizing contribution to the electoral system.

These routines of the individual are similar to those employed by more complex systems. They elevate respect for past decisions to the level of principal consideration in current decisions, and promise stability for the system. The individual's routines show a continuity of party identification over a period of many elections, and within families over several generations; and the use of party identification to color one's view of the environment and ascribe features to ambiguous candidates and issues. Although some people have no stable party identification, and others change party or deviate in their support of its candidates, the routines of party loyalty do seem to be used by most voters in most campaigns. As the title of the chapter indicates, the routines produce a stability of voting and attitudes, and produce sons who resemble their fathers.

In documenting these routines we report first about the stability of party identifications over long periods of time. Then we describe the functioning of a party identification as a cue to interpret the meaning of ambiguous candidates and issues. Finally we describe some mechanisms of political socialization that show how the basic ingredient of these routines—party identification—are transferred from one generation to the next.

The most common observations in studies of voting behavior are that individuals maintain their party identity over many years, and that individuals use party identity to guide their voting behavior and political attitudes. These observations are common enough to be trite. Yet they deserve extensive treatment in this book. They are important political routines, and triteness is one of the features they share with other routines. Like them, the maintenance and use of party identification is an ongoing phenomena that is so obvious it is often ignored in the search for more "significant" or "interesting" causes of behavior. Here we take a close look at the obvious phenomena of stable party identification, explain its role in the political lives of individuals and in the larger political system in which they hold membership, and compare it with other routines that are used by complex organizations.

STABLE PARTY ALLEGIANCES

A stable party identification is one of the features that most Americans maintain throughout their adult lives. Nationwide surveys have attempted to measure the persistence of party identification by asking citizens to recall their first presidential election. One study found that two-thirds of its sample still identified themselves as members of the same party for which they cast their first presidential vote. And a majority of the sample (56 per cent) had *never* deviated from the support of candidates belonging to their initial party.[1]

Party identification is not only strong within one lifetime. It also tends to cement spouses and to remain stable across generations. One survey that asked respondents to recall the party identification of their parents found that 75 percent of the respondents recalled that both parents identified with the same party. Where both parents were Democrats about three-quarters of the children reported that they, too, identified with the Democratic Party; and where both parents were Republican, about 70 percent of the children reported a similar identification.[2]

Individuals often describe their early political memories in homely, poignant ways that testify to the emotional bases of a party loyalty:[3]

My husband was a government employee and we got three cuts in pay under Hoover. We lost our house on account of that.

One thing I don't like when Hoover was President, how I had to work and keep moving on. I remember how in Palm Beach they made me keep on moving. I couldn't get no job. I fell out with the Republicans then.

There's nothing I like about the Republican Party. I remember I didn't get a job from 1929 to 1933. I was healthy and able to work but no job. In those days you had to have a reservation to sleep in the park.

These recollections are made by individuals whose strong identification with the Democratic Party was created—or reinforced—by the hard times of the depression. Other types of recollection also serve to reify party ties. John F. Kennedy once spoke of the hostility he encountered during his early campaign for the Senate, when he passed through towns in western Massachusetts where the only professed Democrat was the town drunk. In these locales the unpleasant image of the Democratic Party helped to maintain local support of the Republican Party. In the South, community leaders once told anti-Republican stories about General Sherman and the Negro governments of Reconstruction.

It would be a mistake to interpret these observations about stable party identification as meaning that citizens invariably vote for the party with which they identify. Actually, the voter's sense of party identification is only one of several factors that influence his choice of candidate. Other determinants include his view of the current situation, the candidates, prominent issues, and the voter's own sense of economic well-being and satisfaction. Party identifications appear to be more stable than voting records. Analysts have developed the concept of the *deviating election* to account for those campaigns won by the party that is usually favored by a minority of voters. The Eisenhower victories of 1952 and 1956 were deviating elections. Despite the Republican majorities at the polls, the Democrats continued to enjoy a majority of party identifications among the respondents to six nation-wide surveys between October 1952 and October 1958.[4] Party identification is itself a variable which can range between strong and weak. The stronger the identification, the more likely is a voter to support his party at the polls. Even where the identification appears to be strong, however, there is a small group of voters who are vulnerable to the situation in the current campaign and liable to cast a deviant vote. A survey taken in 1956 showed that 82 percent of the strong party identifiers voted regularly for the same party, while 60 percent of the weak party identifiers voted regularly for their party.[5]

Although it is rare, some voters actually change their party identifications. About 20–25 percent of a national sample admitted that they changed party affiliation during their lifetime.[6] Of these people, some altered their party in response to changes in their personal lives. The stimuli of personal conversions include moving to a community where the majority of one's contacts are in the opposite party, marriage to a spouse of the opposite party, and the change in a workman's values when he acquires a business of his own. A much larger incidence of conversions has occurred in response to major social forces. The Depression of the 1930s began while the Republicans enjoyed the support of most voters, but the Democrats had won major party status by 1936. Before the Depression the greatest party-realigning trauma was the Civil War. The Republican Party was born during the prewar opposition to slavery and emerged from the War as the major party in the North and West. Before the War southern voters had divided themselves in similar proportions as Northerners, but the experience of Reconstruction left the nation with a solid Democratic South. It is no longer true that Americans describe their party allegiances in terms of slavery and secession, but identifications formed in that context have persisted.

The remoteness of the Civil War prohibits a careful analysis of the party conversions that accompanied it, but the Depression is close enough to permit a detailed study. Middle-age and older survey respondents can answer questions about their political experience during the depression, and provide some basis— perhaps diluted by faults of memory—for understanding party conversions. Their recollections indicate that people who were most likely to change allegiances belonged to marginal demographic groupings that were not subject to strong appeals by their former parties: the young, the poor, and members of minority ethnic groups. The switch made by each group has been the subject of considerable speculation. It may be that the young people were captivated by the "brave new world" character of the Roosevelt Administration, or by its image of social experimentation. Or they may have been repelled by impatience with the outmoded, traditional, and inadequate image of the Republican leadership. It is said that the urban poor were attracted by the substance of Democratic programs. Such policies as support for labor unions, unemployment compensation, public assistance programs, public housing, and the repeal of prohibition are mentioned as the source of new support for Democratic candidates. The members of minority ethnic groups were attracted, supposedly, by Roosevelt's support for the down-trodden. It is reported that Italians found Democratic leaders to be more hospitable than the upper-class Republicans; Negroes welcomed the substance of Democratic programs and grew tired of the Republicans' invocation of Lincoln's heritage; and Jews responded to Roosevelt's opposition to Nazi policies in Europe. The common trait of these groups is a tangential relation to the pre-depression Republican Party. We can surmise that their level of identification with the Republican Party was low, and that they were particularly vulnerable to personal traumas that were brought on by the depression.

In the years since World War II the South appears to have experienced considerable partisan change. Dwight D. Eisenhower won 57 electoral votes in the former Confederacy during 1952, he captured 67 there in 1956, and Richard Nixon won 33 electoral votes from the region during 1960. Barry Goldwater's campaign had a distinctively southern flavor in 1964, 49 of his 53 electoral votes came from the Old South. In 1964, Richard Nixon collected more electoral votes in the South than his Democratic opponent. However, a close inspection of southern politics lessens the view of a Republican upheaval. The party has made almost all of its gains at the presidential level. Several factors have been at work: the apolitical charisma of General Eisenhower, which had its impact on both North and South; the "taint" of Catholicism in the candidacy of John F. Kennedy; and the alienation of Southerners from Lyndon Johnson's civil rights stance in 1964. Survey research failed to show a noticeable change in the party identification of white Southerners during the 1950s.[7] There has been a population replacement in the South which has created highly visible centers of Republican strength where none existed before World War II. While the rural poor (white as well as Negro) have gone north and diluted the strength previously enjoyed by the Democrats, a large number of middle-class Northerners with Republican loyalties have moved to southern cities. These people have been attracted to professional and technical positions in the developing economy. This is particularly true in Florida, where the modern carpetbaggers are joined by a large number of retired people who also bring Republican loyalties. More than any other state in the Old Confederacy, Florida has seen a growth of Republican strength in local, state, and congressional politics, as well as in presidential campaigns.

Among those white Southerners who have admitted a conversion from the Democratic to the Republican Party, the race issue is frequently mentioned as the stimulus. The pro-civil rights posture of the national Democrats has assisted the candidacies of Republican presidential aspirants, and it has also proved an asset to Republican efforts to win state and local positions. Republican candidates for state and local offices attacked the enforcement activities of the U.S. Department of Health, Education and Welfare under the Johnson administration that were directed at the racial integration of schools and hospitals. No matter what the segregationist sentiments of Democratic candidates, they were hard-pressed to avoid the taint of identification with the federal administration. Where well-established office holders themselves switch to the Republican Party—as in the case of Senator Strom Thurmond of South Carolina—they provide the catalyst that carries numerous followers along with them. This principal stimulus of party conversions for white Southerners may also limit the extent to which the South will become a truly two-party political system. For the conversion process to go far beyond its present level, it may be necessary for the Republican Party to make an overt appeal to racist sentiments in the white population. Although this can—and has—occurred in isolated campaigns, it seems unlikely to happen on a systematic basis. Such an effort would embarrass Republicans in the North, where they continue to receive their most concentrated support. Not only would a racist appeal hurt Republican chances among many whites, but it would be disastrous in the party's efforts to recruit among the increasing Negro electorate. Even in the South, well-known conservative Democrats like Senator Herman Talmadge and Governor Lester Maddox have tried to revise their image in the face of a newly-registered Negro electorate.

FACTORS SUPPORTING STABLE PARTY ALLEGIANCE

Several characteristics of American political parties facilitate the maintenance of party loyalties and the use of these loyalties in formulating attitudes about issues and candidates. In particular, the permanence of the parties has provided symbols of long standing with which individuals can identify; and the ideological flexibility of the parties has provided a home within each of them for individuals of various persuasions.

Both of the major parties are old. Their histories pre-date most of the government regimes in "developed" countries. For more than three generations, Americans have been able to think of themselves as Republicans or Democrats. In that time the British have had to accustom themselves to a mass electorate; the French have experienced three military defeats and foreign occupations, plus three Republics; and the Spaniards, Germans, Italians, Russians, Mexicans and Japanese have deposed or severely modified their monarchies. In continuing as viable institutions over the years, the American parties have outlasted their identification with any personalities or events. Each party has its memories of great men and great causes, but neither party has acquired a fixation for the past which has limited its efforts to recruit newcomers and to remain viable. Thus, the parties are more permanent than they might be if they relied on memories of Jackson, Lincoln, Roosevelt, the Civil War, or the Depression in order to keep their voters' loyalties. Although current surveys continue to find residual affection for these symbols among the supporters of each party, it is clear that party affiliations are independent of them. The party celebrations of heroes' birthdays provide innocuous opportunities to enrichen treasuries, but they do not indicate the parties' dependence on the memories of past leaders.

The flexibility of each party's set of "convictions" permits most shades of attitude, belief, and ideology to find a warm reception among like-minded partisans. The multiplicity of beliefs within each party reflects the diverse ways in which groups initially linked themselves with their party. Many families trace their party heritate to the location and beliefs of ancestors who experienced the Civil War and Reconstruction. Others belong to ethnic groups which came to the country between 1880 and 1924, and made a party commitment during the Depression. Many acts of party-identification were formed not out of ideological commitment as much as from following the choice of one's peers. The needs and interests of contemporary adults are different from those of their ancestors who formed the families' political tie. The result is that people adhere to their party because of a variety of reasons, and these reasons do not add up to a coherent picture. The parties are still "open," and their ideological image tends not to scare off potential adherents. Indeed, we see in Chapter VIII that the ideological variety of individual party adherents weakens the parties as disciplined organizations, and makes it difficult for party leaders to develop routines for their own decisions in making nominations, running election campaigns, raising money, or promoting individuals within the party organizations.

The experience of different political streams in the states of Ohio, Indiana, and Illinois testifies to the varieties present in each party and to the ways in which these diversities permit them to recruit and hold people of different beliefs. Each of these states received one stream of early settlers from New York and New England into its northern counties, and another stream of settlers from Maryland, Carolina, and Kentucky who settled in the southern portions. Each stream maintained its prior sectional allegiances after the Civil War. These initial patterns have remained despite considerable cross-county migrations, and the arrival of "outsiders" into all sections. In the northern sections of these states, rural residents continue to show the Republican tendencies resembling those further north and east. In the southern counties, however, rural residents show the Democratic inclinations of the South. The Democratic party serves both urban liberals and rural conservatives, and the Republican party serves urban conservatives and rural liberals. Each party can provide an ideological home for present day liberals or conservatives. And partly because there is no sharp policy differences between the parties, their competition revolves about patronage, jobs, and personalities more than about issues of current policy.[8]

The affiliation of minority ethnic groups to the political parties also insures that each party will continue to attract affiliates of widely-varying political outlooks. The initial party ties of ethnic groups represented a number of linkages aside from ideology. They included the wooing of an ethnic leader by party officials; the efforts of party spokesmen in behalf of an ethnic group or the homeland of the ethnic group; and the economic policies of a party's leaders that coincided with the needs of the ethnic group. In Rhode Island, for example, a link between the Democratic Party and Italian voters was formed partly because John O. Pastore received party support for his own political career.[9] The identification of Franklin Roosevelt as the supporter of European Jews during the Nazi era attracted many Jews to the Party and the identification of Harry Truman with the independence of Israel helped cement these ties. The identification of Abraham Lincoln and with the emancipation of the slaves won early Republican votes among Negroes, but the economic policies identified with the New Deal won many Negroes for the Democrats. Minority ethnic groups no longer exhibit the distinctiveness of their early generations in the United States. It would be a mistake, however, to conclude that the "melting pot" had finished its work and left a uniform culture. Enough residue of ethnic identification remains to provide a basis of party identification. This basis is not ideological as much as it is cultural in nature. The ethnic nature of many individuals' party affiliations works against ideological uniformity within the parties, and facilitates the easy maintenance of a party identification for individuals of all attitudes and beliefs. Party candidates nurture the ethnic loyalties of their constituents by the use of ethnic social groups as campaign audiences, by the use of ethnic phrases or the conspicuous consumption of ethnic foods, and by appropriate pronouncements about relevant domestic issues, or about international issues concerned with the ethnic's homeland.[10] Such appeals insure that each party will remain ideologically diverse and capable of remaining as the affiliation of most Americans.

The maintenance of party identity is important in American politics, but it is not universal. Some data from French survey research indicate that Frenchmen are less likely to develop a firm party affiliation or to pass one on to their children. While 75 percent of American respondents are likely to classify themselves as party affiliates, less than 45 percent of French respondents have done so. And while 85 percent of Americans can identify the party affiliation of their fathers, only 26 percent of Frenchmen comply with questions of this sort.[11] There are several possible interpretations of these findings. Perhaps the multiplicity and fluidity of French parties stand as a barrier to one's firm party identification or the effective passing-on of a parent's affiliation. Or the French may be reluctant to discuss their own political affiliation—either with interviewers or with their children. The result of this reticence would mirror the survey findings: a low incidence of Frenchmen who admit to a party identification, and a low incidence who recall their father's partisanship.[12]

THE USE OF PARTY IDENTIFICATION IN FORMULATING
ATTITUDES TOWARD ISSUES AND CANDIDATES

It is clear from the preceding discussion that most American adults identify themselves readily with one of the major parties, and stay with that party throughout their lives. Also in most cases, theirs is a family party. Affiliation is acquired during childhood and then passed on to the next generation by mature citizens. An individual's party identification is one of the most stable features of American politics.

A stable party allegiance works its influence on politics by helping to shape the attitudes and the voting behavior of party affiliates. Despite the presence of deviating elections, most people who consider themselves to be members of a party vote for that party's candidates most of the time. Party members often make favorable evaluations of personalities who are identified with their party, and contrary evaluations of personalities who are identified with the opposite party. The evidence of party-oriented beliefs may be clearest in those periods of social unrest when citizens are most aware of politics. A 1936 survey asked: *"Do you believe the acts and policies of the Roosevelt Administration may lead to dictatorship?"* Only 9 percent of the Democratic respondents answered this question in the affirmative, while 83 percent of the Republicans answered this way.[13] As noted above, the major parties are flexible enough to include people of diverse ideologies. There is no disciplined obedience to the party line. For most of the people who are only tangentially interested in most issues, however, the prevailing sentiments expressed by party leaders provide useful guides.

For the mass of people who do not take the time to make a careful assessment of political events and personalities, the party is an invaluable guide. Like other routines that we shall examine, one's party allegiance simplifies a complex and ambiguous world. A party label provides a handy tool that identifies the good guys and the bad guys. The party label not only indicates which candidate is likely to be most suitable for a voter, but it also provides guidance in the interpretation of his past record, and the acceptance of comments made about him by newspapers, interest groups, and prominent individuals.[14] The party is most helpful for those people who do not frequently involve themselves in political affairs. Then the clue provided by the party helps the voter evaluate a candidate and his campaign without much competition from other sources of information that he might consider.[15] The function of a party allegiance in a person's political behavior is pictured in Figure III-1.[16] This portrays the flow of influences that impinge on the behaviors of voting, support of a candidate, and advocacy of an issue position. The factors included among the influences are party allegiance; attitudes toward candidates, issues, and interest groups associated with each candidate; current events; social and economic characteristics of the citizen; and his memories about historical events. The items that exert the greatest influence on the ultimate behavior are attitudes relevant to the activity. These attitudes show the strongest statistical relationships with behavior. Where this behavior is a vote, the elements that seem to be most influential are attitudes about the

FIGURE III-1
Party Allegiance and Other Influences on Political Behavior*

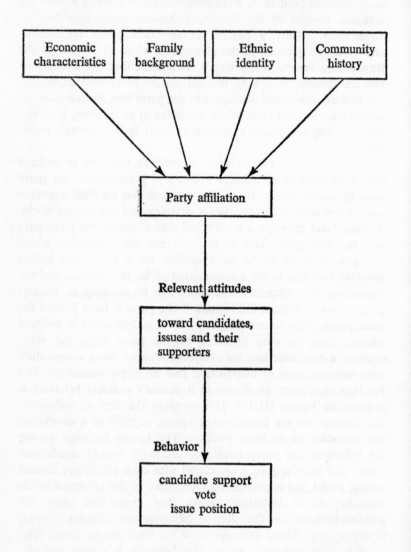

candidate as a person, his issue-positions and the interest groups that are identified with his campaign.

The function of a party allegiance is shown in its influence over the attitudes that lead to behaviors. We know that one's party identification affects one's views of candidates or issues. There is an imperfect correspondence between party allegiance and attitudes. This testifies to the existence of other phenomena that compete with one's party identification for influence over attitudes. Such factors as current events, the posture of a candidate on a sensitive issue, or a recollection about an interest group that is associated with a candidate may occasionally overwhelm contrary messages coming from a party allegiance. "Behind" one's party identification, and more "distant" from political behaviors are the social factors that seem responsible for one's choice of a party. They include family background, ethnic affiliation, and the history of one's community. In the next section of this chapter we shall look more closely at the personal experiences by which individuals acquire their party affiliation. We shall see how each new generation of citizens acquires their party allegiances.

LEARNING PARTY IDENTIFICATION

We noted above that 70–75 percent of the adults acquire their parent's affiliation if both their parents identified with the same party. Along with this data, it is helpful to have some answers to open-ended questions about the origin of one's party tie. The simplicity of these statements, and the matter-of-fact way in which they are reported testify to the naturalness in transmitting party labels at home. The following responses are typical of many that have been recorded.[17]

Well, I was just raised a Republican.

My dad is a Republican and we are all hot Republicans.

I'm from a strong Republican family.

I'm a Democrat; that's what my folks are. No reason otherwise.

Well, my father is a Democrat and I am one by inheritance sort of. I know nothing about politics but I like the Democratic party because I know they are more for the poorer people.

Our forefathers have been Democrats and we have naturally always stuck with the Democratic party.

My folks and family always voted Republican and so I vote Republican.

These statements by adults are complemented by the innocent reply of a young girl to a survey of schoolchildren made in New Haven, Connecticut: "All I know is *we're* not Republicans."[17]

An allegiance to a political party is most prominent among the political traits that youngsters acquire in their homes. Children also acquire a sense of their own roles in the political system, they develop habits of political activity, they learn attitudes about certain political issues, and they acquire information about some prominent institutions of government. Some direct evidence about the policy *opinions of adults and their children toward candidates and issues* shows the expected correspondence. However, this correspondence is lower than that between parents' and children's party identifications.[19] Party is a more visible and unambiguous attachment than an opinion about a political issue, and conversations in the home probably make it more likely that children will identify and take hold of their parents' feelings about the political parties. A party affiliation is also one of the first-learned of a child's political traits. Because of this, it may actually help to condition his later acquisitions and gain reinforcement from the more complex attitudes that he picks up from family and friends.

Because the issues of political controversy change in great detail between the time an adolescent leaves his parents' home and the time of his own political maturity, it is difficult to assess the correspondence between the opinions of adults and their parents. When we look at the opinions of adults who identify themselves with a different social class than they recall for their parents, however, it is apparent that these people show a tendency toward the opinions that would be expected of their parents' social class. Among working class respondents there is a lower incidence of domestic liberalism in the case of those who come from middle-class backgrounds. And among middle-class respondents, there is slightly more liberalism from those with working-class parents.[20] Discussions in the home and in family-related peer groups may plant ideological seeds that subsequent contacts do not erase.

LIMITATIONS OF FAMILY INFLUENCES

Even though the family is important in teaching political routines, it would be improper to end this discussion without some comment about the erosion of family influences. Political learning that occurs within the family circle, or in family-related peer groups is an important element in stabilizing political opinions and alignments in the United States, but it does not impose a rigid barrier against change. Some families are not successful instructors with respect to political attitudes or allegiances. Where the father and mother express contrasting loyalties or beliefs, the offspring is subject to differing influences and is less likely to mirror either his father's or his mother's posture than when both parents express similar opinions. Even where both parents are united politically, the offspring is exposed from his early school years to political messages that differ from those he has heard at home. Especially if he is mobile socially or economically, he will encounter an increasing incidence of disharmonious political messages as he matures and associates with a variety of primary-group contacts. When a person chooses a spouse, he encounters another life-decision that may erode the political identity that he learned from his parents. The political environment of an era can also affect the resilience of political traits acquired from one's parents. A study made in 1952 indicated that respondents under the age of 55 from Democratic families were more likely to have retained their parents' faith than were Republicans. Perhaps the Democratic tenor of the times, reflected principally in the rising stock of that party during the Roosevelt Administration, made it more likely that offspring of Republicans would encounter disharmonious influences and be led from their early loyalties.[21]

SUMMARY AND CONCLUSIONS

The routines described in this chapter serve to perpetuate party loyalties throughout lifetimes and across generations, and lead individuals to evaluate political issues and candidates in terms of their party identification. These may be the most important routines in the electoral system. They add stability and predictability to politics. In America, especially, where party labels have remained the symbols of viable organizations for over a century, allegiances to each major party have dampened swings away from the central tendency of politics, and they have made the voting behavior of large social and economic groups predictable in most contexts. Once the party loyalty is learned by a citizen, it simplifies the complex world of politically-relevant information. Most citizens evaluate candidates according to their party label, and they take positions on current issues according to the party label which each alternatives carries. As a result, the party loyalty helps to isolate the individual—and the larger system of which he is part—from contemporary pressures for change.

A party identity is the earliest and most desirable of political traits that an individual acquires. The party allegiance of parents is relatively simple and unambiguous, especially if mother and father share the same allegiance. Parents who are more involved and informed about politics are most likely to provide their children with political information. By and large, these families are in the middle- and upper-classes. But many lower-class families develop a keen interest in politics, and this compensates for other factors in providing their children with political information. Where the family does teach a good deal of politics to its youngsters, the offspring show early signs of political involvement, and they show a greater-than-usual tendency to employ party loyalties to evaluate current events and personalities.

Each major party has been around long enough to become firmly bedded in family memories. Moreover, the ideological flexibility of the parties permits them to hold on to individuals and families long beyond the time when the issue associated with the first ancestor's conversion became outmoded. Even though party loyalties are durable, they are not strong enough to insure consistent choices of candidates and issue-positions. The party tie must compete with other stimuli when the citizen is assessing current issues and personalities. *Deviating elections* demonstrate that party loyalties may remain firm in the face of wholesale, but temporary, shifts in voters' support. The Presidential elections of 1952 and 1956 are classic examples of deviating elections. President Eisenhower won clear victories, but he had no lasting influence on the basic party loyalties of many people.

Surveys have found that 20–25 percent of the adult population have experienced a political conversion during their lifetimes. Some converts respond to major social upheavals. The Depression affected the party ties of many adults. In a past generation, the Civil War led many individuals to shift party loyalties. Other conversions reflect the influence of personal forces: marriage to a spouse of the opposite party; mobility to a community where one's neighbors differ markedly from one's former contacts; or social-economic mobility that likewise introduces one to a new set of associates.

The reader should realize that the party itself is not the routine that we have discussed. The party is an institution. Routines are aids which citizens use in formulating political attitudes, beliefs, and voting preferences. At the core of these routines are people's attachments to a political party, and their use of the party attachment to guide their evaluation of issues or candidates. The routines lead individuals to make a positive (or negative) evaluation of issues or candidates to the extent that they coincide with (or differ from) cues resulting from their party affiliation. We see in Chapter VIII that *party organizations* are marked by a lack of prominent routines in their own decision-making procedures.

This chapter illustrates two aspects of the analyses that will appear in each of the next four chapters: (1) it is necessary to infer the existence of routines from information that merely shows several factors existing in association with each other; and (2) our claim to the discovery of a routine reflects the observation of general tendencies rather than uniform behaviors. There is no direct evidence that individuals consciously adopt the party loyalties of their parents, or that they consult these loyalties when they formulate opinions about political issues or candidates. We *infer* these routines—which most often are probably not features of conscious deliberation—from the observation that most individuals have the same party identity that they recall from their parents and from their own earlier years, and that individuals usually adopt opinions on issues and candidates that are consistent with their party loyalties. These observations seem accurate most of the time. However, many individuals are without clear party identifications, many change party identifications during their adult years, and many people adopt opinions that are inconsistent with their party identification.

In the following chapters we focus on different kinds of decisions, and we concern ourselves with the actions of formal organizations as well as individuals. As in this chapter, our "discovery" of routines will be based upon inferences; and this discovery will rest upon general tendencies rather than uniform behaviors.

NOTES

1. Angus Campbell, Philip Converse, Warren E. Miller, and Donald Stokes, *The American Voter* (New York: John Wiley, 1960), p. 148.

2. Survey researchers are properly skeptical about the ability of respondents to recall events over long periods of time. In the case of this finding, however, other research techniques find a similar carry-over of party identification from parents to children. See *Ibid.*, p. 147.

3. *Ibid.*, p. 157.

4. *Ibid.*, p. 124.

5. *Ibid.*, p. 125.

6. *Ibid.*, p. 150.

7. Angus Campbell, Philip Converse, Warren E. Miller, and Donald Stokes, *Elections and the Political Order* (New York: John Wiley, 1964), p. 225.

8. John H. Fenton, *Midwest Politics* (New York. Holt, Rinehart and Winston, 1966).

9. Samuel Lubell, *The Future of American Politics* (Garden City: Anchor Books, 1956).

10. Michael Parenti, "Ethnic Politics and the Persistence of Ethnic Identification," *American Political Science Review*, LXI (September 1967), pp. 717–26).

11. *Elections and the Political Order, op.cit.*, p. 277ff.

12. *Ibid.*, p. 281.

13. V. O. Key, *Public Opinion and American Democracy* (New York: Alfred A. Knopf, 1961), p. 246.

14. *American Voter, op.cit.*, p. 128.

15. *Ibid.*, p. 136.

16. The chart is derived from *The American Voter, op. cit.*, pp. 24–32.

17. Key, *op. cit.*, pp. 297–98.

18. Fred I. Greenstein, *Children and Politics* (New Haven: Yale University Press, 196?), p. 73.

19. *Ibid.*, p. 306.

20. Key, *op. cit.*, p. 308.

21. Key, *op. cit.*, p. 301.

IV.   Incremental Budgeting

INCREMENTAL BUDGETING IS A POLITICAL ROUTINE THAT MAY BE
the archetype of all others. In its acceptance of previous levels of
expenditure for its primary decision criteria, incrementalism simplifies the decision process. Its practitioners tend to accept requests for spending that will support established program, and
they tend to cut sharply any requests for large budget increases.
The whole range of habits, previous accommodations among antagonists, and established public services escape notice of officials
as they concentrate upon the increment of change that is requested in an agency's budget. Incrementalism serves to isolate its
practitioners from the larger social system, and the current demands, resources, and supports that are relevant to unexamined
budget items. Where officials consider nothing to be so legitimate
as their own past actions, it is likely that a minimum of stimuli will
penetrate into their decision arena. The stabilizing effect of incrementalism is obvious. The budgets of most agencies inch upward
over the years. Nothing short of a major social or economic crisis
seems able to cause a major alteration. The advocates of major
new programs make their case with legislative committees rather
than with appropriations committees, and it is often decided to
create new agencies to handle the innovations. In this way the
programs will not be tied to the budget-makers' disinclination to
permit the budget of an established agency to show an unusual
spurt of growth. An understanding of incremental budgeting is
essential for students of public finance. No factor shows as close a
correspondence with current expenditures as does the level of
previous expenditures. Although budgets do change over time,
they tend to show orderly and uniform rates of change. When
individual agencies increase their budgets at an unusually high
rate, they suggest the presence of powerful underlying stimuli in
politics or economics.

INCREMENTAL BUDGETING IN THE FEDERAL GOVERNMENT

The use of incremental budgeting in the federal government is
evident in the participants' fixation on the base of expenditures

that has been established by earlier decisions. Conversations among the participants focus on percentages. Agency personnel are concerned with the percentage increase they should request; reviewers in the departmental budget offices and the Bureau of the Budget calculate their actions in terms of percentage cuts to be imposed on the agencies' requests; Congressmen on the House Appropriations Committee discuss their own percentage changes in the President's Budget; and their counterparts in the Senate talk about the percentage changes they will make in the House decision. Each of the participants also calculates from the prime base—the agency's previous appropriation. Many administrators in the agencies want to increase this base, while reviewers in the department, in the Budget Bureau and in Congress reckon themselves successful if they hold the line close to this base. One observer of the federal budget process summarizes these behaviors in the labels given to three principal budget strategies:[1]

1. Defending the base; guarding against cuts in the old programs
2. Increasing the base: inching ahead with existing programs
3. Expanding the base: adding new programs

Incremental budgeting is not a simple routine that can be described with a single decision rule. More accurately, it is a complex of subroutines that differ in specific rules while they share a clear theme. That theme is: previous decisions are generally legitimate; concentrate the investigation on deviations that are requested.

The "previous decisions" that are at issue in federal budgeting vary with each stage of the budget process. The treatment of the "increment" that is requested also varies—with the stage of the budget process, with the nature of the political environment, with the character of the agency that is at issue, and with the opinions of the reviewers. In one study of budget histories for 56 agencies during the 1947–63 period, the following decision-rules were found to be prominent:[2]

1. The average agency request[3] for a certain year is a fixed percentage of the Congressional appropriation for that agency in the previous year plus a random variable for that year.

2. The average agency request for a certain year is a fixed percentage of the Congressional appropriation for that agency in the previous year plus a mean percentage of the difference between the

Congressional appropriation and the agency request for the previous year plus a random variable for that year.

3. The average agency request for a certain year is a fixed percentage of the agency's request for the previous year plus a random variable for that year.

4. The average Congressional appropriation for an agency in a certain year is a fixed percentage of the agency's request in that year, plus a random variable for that year.

5. The average Congressional appropriation for an agency is a fixed percentage of the agency's request for that year plus a random variable representing a deviation from the usual relationship between Congress and the agency in the previous year plus a random variable for the current year.

6. The average Congressional appropriation for an agency is a fixed percentage of the agency's request for a certain year plus a fixed percentage of the agency's request for the year at issue which is not part of the appropriation or request of the previous year plus a random variable representing the part of the appropriation attributable to the special circumstances of the year.

The first, third and fourth of these decision rules are simple responses to a previous action and the prevailing climate. Rules 2, 5, and 6 are more complicated gaming strategies that seek to adjust current decisions for previously unmet desires as well as to the current climate and the level of expenditure defined in the previous decision. The combination of strategies that is used most often is the relatively simple 1 followed by 4. Agencies occasionally follow with 3 when Congress has appropriated all, or almost all, the request that had been made during the preceeding year. Thus, participants in federal budgeting may have alternate "bases" from which to begin their incremental calculations. They often begin from the base which is most favorable to their present desires.

These decision rules only depict frequently-used routines in federal budgeting. They do not represent the full universe of budget cases. Among the instances observed when agency budgets deviated from the rules, most followed changes in the party complexion of the Presidency and Congress. During the 80th Congress (1947–48), newly-empowered Republicans made a special effort to reduce the budgets that were submitted by the Democratic President. Many unusual budget decisions occurred during the early Eisenhower years of 1953–55, and the Kennedy-Johnson years of 1962–63. When the deviating budgets are examined individually, the largest number reflect significant changes in the substance of agency programs. Other circumstances include changes in fiscal policy and a felt need for increased agency-supervision among Congressmen.

A continuing controversy in incremental budgeting concerns the size of the increment. It is routine that calculations begin from the base of a previous budgetary decision, but it is less regular that the size of the increment is stable from one period of time to another, or from one actor to another within a year's budget cycle. A second study of federal budgeting—covering 36 agencies during the 1947–62 period—provides some information about the increments that were voted.[4]

As might be expected, the spenders in the federal government typically request larger increments than budget-reviewers will grant. Twenty-four of the 36 agencies made annual requests that averaged at least 10 percent above previous appropriations, 11 made annual requests that averaged at least 20 percent above their previous appropriations, and the annual requests of two averaged at least 75 percent above earlier funds. In contrast, the Appropriations Committee in the House of Representatives permitted annual growth rates in excess of ten percent for only 12 of the agencies, and an annual growth rate in excess of 20 percent for only one of them.[5]

The Appropriations Committee in the Senate typically serves as a court of appeals to the House decisions. It concentrates on the grievances that agencies hold after their House experience, and it typically adds to the House grant. The House appropriation is the *base* that the Senate works from, and the increment between the House and Senate figure is usually small. For only ten of the 36 agencies did the Senate provide an average 5 percent more of its request than did the House, and for only two of the agencies was the Senate's generosity as much as 10 percent above the House. The Senate was most generous with the agencies that suffered the worse cuts in the House Committee. Much of this generosity was focused on agencies in the Department of the Interior, which had few patrons on the House Committee but considerable support on the Senate Committee. Nevertheless, the Senate Committee did not vote more than an average 9 percent above the House for any of these favored agencies.[6]

Although there is some pulling and hauling of each agency's budget between the House and the Senate, neither body departs markedly from the request for each agency that is included in the President's Budget. Twenty-seven out of 36 agencies emerged from the Senate with appropriations within an average 5 percent of the President's requests during the 1947–62 period, and 35 of the agencies had appropriations within an average 10 percent of requests. Only one agency experienced budget changes in Congress that averaged more than 10 percent. The appropriation of the National Bureau of Standards came out of the House Committee with an average 84.2 percent of requests, and then moved up to an average 87.2 percent in the Senate Committee.[7] In the next chapter we return to the legislature's reliance on the budget cues of executives, and describe certain features that make it a routine distinct from incremental budgeting.

INCREMENTAL BUDGETING IN STATE GOVERNMENTS

State governments provide a useful laboratory for the observation and analysis of incremental budgeting. Their many agencies and diverse economic, social, and political environments provide opportunities for several variants of incremental budgeting to show themselves. And the multiplicity of conditions provides the opportunity to see what types of situation give rise to which varieties of incrementalism.

As in federal budgeting, the common ingredient of incrementalism in state governments is a fixation upon previously made decisions. When administrators in state agencies plan their requests, their paperwork requires them to list current and previous expenditures, and to compare these figures with their estimates for the coming year. Moreover, agency personnel must justify their increment of increase with respect to the guidelines announced by superiors. These guidelines typically estimate the increases in revenue that are expected, or they indicate the priorities to be given individual programs. Last year's budget has the greatest legitimacy in the eyes of governors, central budget officers, and members of legislative appropriations committees. It represents the funds considered necessary to operate established programs, and these funds tend to escape current review. Budget examiners are most likely to question the funds that would increase appropriations, and they are most likely to cut from these requests in order to minimize budget growth.

If anything can be said about the differences in incremental budgeting at state and federal levels, it is that state personnel seem to be even more fascinated with the dollar-increment of change in an agency's budget proposal. Studies of the federal budget process indicate that budget reviewers often question the substance of programs that are to be purchased with the budget increment. One study of state decision-makers, however, indicates that there is a narrow fixation on the dollar amount of the increment, with virtually no attention paid to the substance of the program that is at issue.[9] There are several possible explanations for the narrower inquiry that proceeds at the state level. Personnel in the central budget offices of state governments have fewer investigatory resources than do their counterparts in the U.S. Bureau of the Budget, so their inquiry must be more cursory. In the state legislature, there is less staff assistance than in the U.S. Congress, and the members of appropriations committees are themselves less well prepared to make a detailed investigation of agency programs. Many state legislatures do not have the well-developed seniority system that prevails in Congress, so the members of appropriations committees are likely to be new—and inexperienced—at their work. Moreover, state legislatures suffer from high rates of turnover; there is often a 40 percent loss of membership at each election. This turnover is largely voluntary and it reflects the low prestige enjoyed by state legislators in the political system.

The concern of state budget-makers with their own past decisions is evident in the correspondence between most states' level of spending in one year and its level in earlier years. This is not to say that state governments remain at fixed levels of spending. Revenues and expenditures increase in most years. However, most states' spending increases at about the same rate as their budget-makers show similar disinclinations to move upward rapidly. The result is that states tend to remain at the same levels of spending—relative to one another—from one budget period to the next.[10]

As time increases between any two sets of expenditure decisions, there is increasing opportunity for factors to enter the process that are remote from the first budget. When budget makers prepare for their current decisions, they generally examine only the appropriation of the present or the immediate past. Yet even as the time between a current budget period and a year in the past increases, the expenditures of that past year retain their status of legitimacy; they are part of the nucleus around which later activities (and expenditures) have grown. In 1965, many state governments were spending at positions relative to other states that were similar to their position in 1903. Despite several major wars and transformations in the economy, together with vast population changes in some of the western and southern states and an increase of many-fold in the magnitude of each state's spending, the basic pattern of states' spending has remained similar throughout the century. States that were high (or low) spenders in 1903 have generally remained high (or low) spenders until the present.

Incremental budgeting is not equally conservative in all fields of government activity. During the 1957–62 period, spending levels of the states remained most consistent in the fields of education, public welfare, and general government, and least consistent in the highway field. These differences reflect the nature of program changes occurring in these fields during the 1957–62 period. There were great changes in highway expenditures stimulated by federal money for the Interstate and Defense Highway system. Some states took advantage of these federal funds more rapidly than other, and the 1962 pattern of spending differed from that of 1957. Spending patterns for general government show the greatest stability over the 1957–62 period. This reflects the inert nature of activities. The budget for general government supports the Legislature and Judiciary (22 percent of the funds in 1962), employment security administration (35 percent), and financial administration (45 percent). Compared to other areas of state government activity, these fields have escaped vast substantive changes. Likewise, spending patterns in the field of public welfare remained stable during the 1957–62 period. This finding may reflect the resistance to innovation among professional welfare administrators that has been cited for the period before 1962.[11] Spending patterns in education also remained stable during the 1957–62 period. While education budgets increased faster than the average during 1957–62 (19 percent increase in education and 15 percent increase in total spending), this did not upset state positions in spending for education. Perhaps educational administrators are sufficiently attuned to new developments so that most states adopt innovations (and increase spending) at about the same rate. The result would mirror the present findings: great increases in educational expenditures along with stability of interstate differences between 1957 and 1962.

The examination of aggregate state government expenditures shows the importance of previous expenditures in government budgeting, but it does not detail the ways in which specific actors respond to one another's decisions. By looking at relationships between the nature of agency requests, the governor's recommendations to the legislature, and the subsequent actions of the legislature, we can see how the governor and the legislature actually make their budget decisions in an incremental fashion.[12]

Administrative agencies and the governor play the most consistent roles in the state budget process. In each of nineteen states reported in Table IV-1, the agencies requested a sizable increase (15–53 percent) over their current appropriations for the coming year and the governor pared the increase in his recommendations (by 4–31 percent). Agencies requested an average 24 percent increase over their current budgets, and the governor's recommendation trimmed an average 14 percent from their requests. The legislature's final appropriation typically remained close to the governor's recommendation, but varied from a cut of 8 percent below his recommendation to an increase of 19 percent above his recommendation. Six of the legislatures cut agency budgets below the governor's figure, and eleven appropriated more than the governor asked. In only one case, however, did a legislature (in Nebraska) give more money to the agencies than they had requested themselves. The average legislative grant for the coming period was 13 percent below the agencies' request, but 13 percent above the agencies' current budget.

When we examine the response of governors and legislatures to the budgets of individual agencies, we find that the *acquisitiveness* of the agency requests plays a crucial role in the decision of other budget-makers. In most of the states examined, the governor and

TABLE IV-1

Average Annual Percentage Changes at Major Stages in the Budget Process, by State

State, showing years of budget analyzed	Agency request as percent of current expenditure	Governor's recommendation as a percent of agency request	Legislature's appropriation as a percent of Gov's request	Legislature's appropriation as a percent of agency's current Legislature's	Legislature's appropriation as a percent of expenditure agency request
Florida 1965–67	120	90	93	109	84
Georgia 1965–67	153	86	100	139	87
Idaho 1967–69	119	93	92	109	86
Illinois 1963–65	118	83	102	108	85
Indiana 1965–67	123	83	103	112	86
Kentucky 1966–68	120	90	93	109	84
Louisiana 1966–67	121	90	101	110	91
Maine 1965–67	114	85	108	109	92
Nebraska 1965–67	122	87	119	124	104
North Carolina 1965–67	120	84	105	112	87
North Dakota 1965–67	124	74	111	111	82
South Carolina 1966–67	117	96	104	116	99
South Dakota 1967–68	136	82	98	109	80
Texas 1965–67	128	82	104	117	86
Vermont 1965–67	121	87	106	115	91
Virginia 1966–68	120	92	100	114	91
West Virginia 1966–67	125	88	92	101	81
Wisconsin 1965–67	115	96	98	111	94
Wyoming 1967–69	133	69	109	112	75

Source: Ira Sharkansky, "Agency Requests, Gubernatorial Recommendations and Budget Success in State Legislatures," *American Political Science Review*, LXII (December, 1968).

legislature direct the greatest percentage cuts at the agencies that request the greatest percentage increases. However, it is only these acquisitive agencies that come out of the legislature with substantial increases over their previous budgets. Both the governor and the legislature are using similar decision rules: *cut the agencies that ask for a large increase; but do not recommend a budget expansion for those agencies that ask for no increase.* The absolute size of agency budget requests does not appear to influence the decisions made by the governor or legislature. Budget reviewers in the governor's office and the legislature are more likely to respond to the *percentage increment of change that is requested* (i.e., agency acquisitiveness) than to the sheer size of the request.

The failure of either the governor or the legislature to impose additional funds on those agencies which do not ask for them illustrates how much the incremental budget makers depend on someone else taking the initiative in policy innovation. Budget reviewers in the governor's office and the legislature have let this initiative pass over to the agencies. This is part of the often-observed shift in the locus of innovation from elected officials to professionals. It is said to reflect the increasing technological sophistication of public services, and the need for professional training in order to comprehend the public's needs or to design alterations in current programs. It is consistent with their other traits that incremental budget-makers expect recommendations for policy-change to come out of the agencies. Their incremental routine itself represents a reluctance to control policy in a comprehensive fashion through the medium of the budget.

Because agency acquisitiveness shows similar relationships with both the governor's recommendation and the legislature's appropriation, one is tempted to ask if the legislature responds directly to the agencies acquisitiveness, or merely to the governor's recommendation. The results of a causal analysis[13] support the inference that the legislature responds more often to the governor's recommendations than directly to agency acquisitiveness. Only in the cases of South Dakota, Texas, and Virginia does the legislature show some tendency to make an independent assessment of agency request. We return to these findings in the next chapter and focus attention on the separate routine of legislative reliance on executive budget cues.

VARIATIONS IN INCREMENTAL BUDGETING

The routines of incremental budgeting lead reviewers to reduce the estimate of growth-oriented bureaus, and to withhold increases from the bureaus that have not sought more funds. Nevertheless, these decision-rules are not uniform. Some governors and legislatures are more or less likely than their counterparts in other states (or in their states during other years) to grant or withhold funds to agencies that request increments. By examining the nature of budget relationships between agencies, the governor and the legislature in conjunction with several other characteristics of each state, we can gain some insight into the elements that influence budget decisions. Actually, the findings are not crystal clear. Although some relationships prevail between the nature of budget decisions and several traits of the state's politics and economy, there are many instances of budget decisions that do not correspond to the general patterns. Variations from incremental budget routines are not governed by objective forces of economics or politics. Instead they appear to develop individually in the context of each state.

Two characteristics associated with strong gubernatorial restraint against agency budget development are his possession of strong formal veto powers, and high state government expenditures. The already high expenditures may incline the governor against further large increases in state spending, and the power of a veto may strengthen the governor's resolve to impose a severe review on the agencies when they submit requests to him. Where the governor is unusually generous toward agency requests for budget expansion, there tends to be relatively intense party competition. A competitive party situation may lead him to advance his own career—and his party—by supporting innovative agencies.

Where the legislature is particularly restrictive against agency budget development there tends to be relatively high state government expenditure and debt, and a low incidence of state officials who are separately elected. Like the governor, the legislature appears to resist an acquisitive agency in the face of already-committed state resources (i.e., high expenditures and debt). With a scarcity of separately elected executives, agency heads may lack for politically independent allies who can promote their budget through the legislature.

CHANGES IN GOVERNMENT SPENDING: ERUPTIONS IN THE
INCREMENT

The role of incrementalism in state budgeting is one that sets
outside limits to the percentage of change that is feasible, instead
of one that defines precisely the direction and magnitude of the
change that will occur. An examination of budget-changes during
eleven periods between 1903 and 1965 found only weak patterns
between the magnitude of change in each state's spending and its
expenditures in an earlier year.[14] It is not possible to predict the
level of expenditures in a forthcoming year simply by knowing the
current level of expenditure. Although most states' expenditures
in year $a + i$ are close to the same relative positions as they were
in year a, the direction and magnitude of change is not consistent.
Several states go up slightly in their spending, others may drop, a
few demonstrate sizable changes in position, and many maintain
their same position during the period. Major exceptions to these
findings occurred during 1929–39 and 1962–65. Then there were
clear patterns of correspondence between spending in the first
year of each period and the direction and magnitude of change.
In the decade of the depression, the low spending states showed
consistently greater increases in spending than the high spending
states, and the gap between high and low spenders lessened
considerably. This may have been the product of several new
federal aid programs that were started during the Depression,
partly in order to redistribute resources between "have" and
"have not" states. During the 1962–65 period, in contrast, the
high spending states showed consistently greater increases and the
gap widened between high and low spenders.

One of the factors that holds state governments in their same
relative spending positions for many years at a time is their
inability to support marked increases in spending (relative to the
increases of other states) over a span of several budget periods.
States that show considerable increase in one period display decrease or stability (relative to other states) in a following period.
The study of 11 different periods between 1903 and 1965 found
pronounced fluctuations in the rate of change in the spending of
individual states. The long-term increase in a state's spending
occurs in spurts. A period of relative increase follows a period of
stability or decline with respect to the general upward trend.

These fluctuations in state expenditures suggest that officials are unable or unwilling to make continued sharp increases in expenditures. Perhaps after a period of increase, legislators show a limited tolerance for budgets that seek additional growth, or agency heads encounter problems in the continuing process of expanding their operations. Their problems include personnel recruitment, organizational adjustments, changes in agencies' relations with their clients and with legislative and executive overseers. After an increase in expenditures administrators might try to consolidate gains without seeking budget increases, or legislators might slash whatever proposed increases come before them. After a period of relative stability, however, certain legislators, interest groups, and administrators may build widespread support for budgetary advances. The alternation between expenditure increase and stability may also reflect the processes of an administration's muturation. A governor or agency head may come into office with new ideas. But after certain program changes (and increases in expenditures) the new administration may exhaust its ideas or political energies. Innovation will then cease to be the dominant orientation, and expenditure stabilization will follow after budget increases.

Although incremental routines generally isolate budget-makers from the continuing influence of environmental factors, certain rare national trauma have also left their influence upon government budgets. Table IV-2 presents several kinds of data that will facilitate the identification and analysis of these influences. It

TABLE IV-2

Combined Federal, State and Local Government Spending per Capita (in 1954 dollars), 1932–62

	Total spending	Common function domestic spending
1962	$731.90	$329.28
1955	648.30	256.48
1953	701.49	235.21
1950	536.00	250.55
1944	1,253.02	211.47
1940	341.94	239.91
1936	297.09	233.52
1932	252.73	177.18

shows changes in government spending from 1932 to 1962, in total and for "common function" domestic services, corrected for changes in population and inflation.[15]

Since 1932 there have been several unusual increases in government spending, and several instances of expenditure decline. Both types of episode require our attention. The periods of unusual growth signal pressures that stretched the magnitude of increments. Even more startling are the occasional periods of general decline in expenditures. These indicate that certain pressures force budget-makers to reexamine and cut the programs that are funded with the existing level of spending.

The total spending of all governments in the United States increased slowly during the Depression, multiplied by four times during World War II, declined between the War's end and the Korean Conflict (but not to the prewar level), increased again during the Korean War, declined afterward (but again not to the prewar level), and then continued to increase slowly.

The spending increases of the Depression were most dramatic during 1934–36. Spending for natural resources and public welfare provided the major components of these increases. Congress passed a series of new grant-in-aid programs designed to soften effects of the depression: surplus commodity distribution, soil conservation, price parity, old age assistance, aid to families with dependent children, aid to the blind, and child welfare.

Although the Second World War and the Korean Conflict saw great increases in total spending, there was a sharp initial drop in *domestic* spending during each war, followed by moderate increases. The decrease in domestic spending reflects the scarcity of resources brought about by the wars. Manpower, capital equipment, and materials became less available for civilian purposes and precluded many opportunities for state, local, and federal agencies to spend at previous levels. The number of non-federal government employees *declined* by 174,000 between 1940 and 1944. The wars also affected receipts from federal aids. In 1940–42 state and local receipts from federal aid decreased $87 million. War-time losses in spending for public welfare also reflected declines in the number of clients for public assistance. The economic activity generated by the war made jobs available to people who had been unemployed. The mobilization of servicemen cut into college enrollments and the pool of male school teachers, and the scarcity of building materials reduced school construction; all these factors permitted reductions in spending for education.[16] As this book goes to press, the war in Viet Nam appears to be having similar influences on both total government spending, and that for domestic services. As in past wars, total Federal spending is increasing—largely to pay the war costs—while state and local governments face great difficulties in meeting their past commitments. At the present time, however, it is not feasible to compare in precise terms the present experience to that of World War II or Korea.

In postwar years, total spending has declined (reflecting the cutback of military activities) but domestic spending surged ahead. The availability of manpower for domestic purposes supported these increases. From 1946 to 1962 state and local government employees per 10,000 population increased by 46 percent. The need to make up for postponed repairs and new construction, to provide for a growth in population and work-loads stimulated increases in tax effort and federal aids. State and local taxes increased from 5.6 to 9.4 percent of personal income during 1946–62 and federal grants increased from 5.7 to 12.8 percent of state and local revenue. Congress added significant new federal aid programs for federally-impacted school districts, national defense education, and interstate highways. Population increases required vast capital expenditures for new primary schools during the late 1940s. Gradually the war babies advanced through the grades to college and graduate school. They have also added to demands for public hospitals, correctional institutions, recreational facilities and highways. At each stage of their lives, babies from World War II and Korea (and now their children) have stimulated increases in local, state, and federal budgets.

INCREMENTAL BUDGETING AND THE POLITICAL SYSTEM

More clearly than other routines which operate in the policy-making process, incremental budgeting plays a conservative role in the political system. The preoccupation of budget-makers with their own past decisions makes it unlikely that any stimulus of change will have a revolutionary impact on their decisions. While it is true that environmental conditions do intrude upon the budgeting arena, it is apparent that the incremental routine serves to hold most governmental units at a fixed spending position in relation to other units. Although state spending levels changed noticeably during the depression, World War II and the postwar reconversion, the spending positions of most states (relative to one another) remained at similar levels throughout each of these periods. While budget-makers responded to these severe pressures, they kept an eye on the base of their previous expenditures, and moved from that position. None of the national crises of this century was powerful enough to wholly upset the established positions of states' spending.

The "distance" in responsiveness between budget-making and other features of politics or economics does not hold much promise for the use of budgeting as a vehicle for major change in the United States. While spending decisions occasionally have telling influence upon external phenomena, the nature of budgeting criteria make success unlikely for any particular effort. The reformer must be an optimist as he approaches a public budgetmaker with a vision of change. As they have been described by several observers, the participants in government budgeting are guided not so much by compelling program sympathies as by their own past decisions.

What are the prospects of change in the budget mechanisms themselves? How good are the chances for a reformer who seeks to oust incrementalism from decision making procedures? Can the rational-comprehensive style with its consideration of every budget item and all cogent alternatives become operational?

As suggested by their use by so many budget-makers, the routines of incremental budgeting probably satisfy many officials at all levels of government. Budget processes that respect the past may have a peculiar appeal in the midst of the ongoing pluralistic struggle for changes in American society. As a conservative bulwark the budget may permit legislators, administrators and private groups to tolerate competition for change because no "radical" change is likely to survive the funding process. If the mechanics of budgeting change, it is possible that budget-makers (with the encouragement of outsiders) will operate a new machine essentially as they operate now with the base and incrementalism.[17]

No assessment of possible changes in budgeting procedures can fail to reckon with its complex techniques. There is a lead-time of many months within the budgeting process. At the federal level 27 months elapse between the beginning of budget-making and the end of the fiscal year.[18] In states with biennial appropriations the gap between the agencies' first decisions about their requests and final expenditures is considerably longer. Within this span of time actors operate formally under authority derived from several statutes or executive orders and informally under procedures devised by legislators and administrators. They fill the time with highly technical paperwork and a number of deadlines.[19] Laymen do not seem anxious to learn the innards of budgeting. The mystery of budgeting and its removal from public controversy may be among the factors that makes the outputs of current spending so important later on as inputs for subsequent decisions.

Although no reformers have succeeded in ridding government budgeting of incrementalism, there has been no end of attempts at modification. Several efforts have coincided with the crises of war and economic depression, and provide further evidence for the proposition that it is critical social and economic events that bring about derivations from political routines. The most current effort at budget reforms is "Planning-Programming-Budgeting Systems," often labelled "PPBS." This is actually a complex set of processes. It includes the systems analysis of service-producing units, and estimates of "cost-effectiveness" ratios for each way of providing service. While it is too early to guess whether ppbs will take over from incrementalism, there is little optimism among political scientists. We shall assess PPBS and other attempts at budget reforms more fully in Chapter X, where we focus on the factors capable of changing routines.

SUMMARY AND CONCLUSION

Incremental budgeting is the first policy-making routine to be examined in this book, and in several respects it is an archetype. It helps public officials to *simplify* the issues in budget-making by focusing their attention on the increment that separates the current proposal from the expenditures that have been legitimated by previous decisions. Incrementalism also serves to *isolate* the policy-maker from his environment. By legitimating his own past actions and accepting them as given, the decision-maker excuses himself from considering many aspects of current demands, supports, and resources. For the political scientist, incremental budgeting provides a proximate explanation for government spending: current spending seldom varies markedly from an agency's previous budget because budget-makers usually permit only small increments of change. Finally, deviations from incremental budgeting offer insight to these aspects of the political process that generate basic departures from business as usual.

The decisions of incrementalists focus both on the previous appropriations of a governmental unit, and on the previous decisions that have been made in the current budget sequence. At the federal level, members of the House Appropriations Committee fix their calculations on the recommendations of the Bureau of the Budget, and members of the Senate Appropriations Committee gear their own choices to those of the House of Representatives. Congressional appropriations typically are lower than are the recommendations passed on to Congress by the Budget Bureau. At the state level, the findings are not so clear. Legislators tend to take their own cues from the governor's recommendations, but in about one-half of the states investigated, the legislature tends to give the agencies more funds than the governor recommends.

The incremental nature of state government budgeting is evident in the stability of each state's spending position relative to those of other states. The interstate spending differentials of 1965 bear very close resemblance to those of the recent past, and they show some similarities to the spending patterns of six decades past. The historical factors of Depression, war, and postwar reconversion left their mark on the level of state expenditures. But these factors had less of an impact on interstate differentials in spending. The persistence of these differentials testifies to the reluctance of state officials to depart too markedly from their base of previous expenditures, no matter what the environmental conditions. During most periods, state expenditures move upward in spurts. A period of stability usually alternates with a period of relative increase, thus keeping each state from departing too much from its earlier spending position relative to other states. The base of previous expenditures sets limits within which environmental conditions may affect the precise nature of change during a budget period.

The behavioral manifestations of incremental budgeting are evident in the relationships between the requests of state agencies, recommendations of the governor, and appropriations voted by the legislature. The sheer size of an agency's request is less important for other actors than is the size of increment that it requests. Both the governor and the legislature react negatively in the short run to an acquisitive agency, but they only give increases to those agencies which ask for them. Both findings reveal the conservative bias of incremental budgeting. Its practitioners cut the requests that seek sizable increases, and they seldom force an increase upon any unit that has not asked for it.

The routine to be considered in the next chapter—the legislature's reliance on the executive's budget cues—is similar to incrementalism. The legislature typically responds to earlier actions in the budget sequence. However, this second routine warrants separate treatment. It highlights a weakness in the legislative segment of the budget process that may reflect weakness in a wider range of the legislature's activity. The typical state legislature does not make its own assessment of an agency's budget request. It takes the advice of the chief executive as a primary cue, and votes a budget that is close to his recommendation.

NOTES

1. Aaron Wildavsky, *The Politics of the Budgetary Process* (Boston: Little, Brown, 1964), Chapter 3.

2. Otto A. Davis, M. A. H. Dempster, and Aaron Wildavsky, "A Theory of the Budgetary Process," *American Political Science Review*, LX (September 1966), pp. 529–47.

3. In this research, the limitations of the data require that recommendations of the Bureau of the Budget be equated with the "agency request," *loc. cit.*

4. Richard F. Fenno, Jr., *The Power of the Purse: Appropriations Politics in Congress* (Boston: Little, Brown, 1966).

5. *Ibid.*, Chapter 8.

6. *Ibid.*, Chapter 11.

7. *Ibid.*, p. 585.

8. This section relies on material to be found in my *Spending in the American States* (Chicago: Rand McNally, 1968); and "Agency Requests, Gubernatorial Recommendations and Budget Success in State Legislatures," *American Political Science Review*, LXII (December 1968).

9. Thomas J. Anton, *The Politics of State Expenditure in Illinois* (Urbana: University of Illinois Press, 1966), pp. 253–55.

10. This discussion relies on my *Spending in the American States, op. cit.,* Chapter III.

11. Gilbert Y. Steiner, *Social Insecurity: The Politics of Welfare* (Chicago: Rand McNally, 1966).

12. See my article cited in note #8 above.

13. For details of this analysis, see my article cited in #8 above.

14. See my *Spending in the American States, op. cit.,* Chapter III.

15. The data correct for changes in population and inflation in order to screen out those increases in spending that merely represent the governments' need to spend more dollars in order to allocate economic resources of the same value (perhaps defended to the legislature as "the price increases that are affecting everyone"), and the need to spend more money to provide an unchanging level of service to a growing clientele. "Common function" expenditures support domestic services that federal, state, and local governments provide in common. Eliminated from "total expenditures" are money for defense and international relations, interest on the national debt, space exploration, and the postal service. The following analysis draws upon my *The Politics of Taxing and Spending* (Indianapolis: Bobbs-Merrill, 1969), Chapter V.

16. The low birth rates of the 1930's also lessened the pressure for elementary school spending in the early 1940's.

17. Aaron Wildavsky, "Political Implications of Budgetary Reform," *Public Administration Review,* XXI (Autumn 1961), pp. 183–90.

18. See my *The Politics of Taxing and Spending, op. cit.,* Chapter III.

19. Anton, *op. cit.,* pp. 236–40.

V. Legislators' Reliance on the Executive's Budget Cues

IN THE PREVIOUS DISCUSSION OF INCREMENTAL BUDGETING, WE described the tendency of budget-makers to base their calculations upon the decisions made by the prior actor in the process. Agency officials start many of their calculations from the appropriation that was voted by the legislature during the previous year; the central budget office and the executive respond primarily to the request which has been made by the agency; and the legislature gears its decisions to the recommendation of the executive. Each of these decisions are part of incrementalism. The actors focus on the decision which is just made, and attempt to keep their own recommendation within a certain range of that decision. The overall effect is that agency budgets grow in an orderly fashion, with very few agencies showing large increases in expenditure from one budget period to the next.

In this chapter we focus on one part of this incremental process that has received little attention previously. The legislators' reliance on the executive's budget cues is a routine that is distinct in certain ways from other elements of incrementalism. The legislators begin their calculations from the executive's recommendations partly to realize a prime goal of incrementalism (i.e., to minimize expenditure-growth). However, there are separate reasons for accepting the executive's recommendations that grow out of peculiarities in the legislators' working conditions.

FACTORS DISCOURAGING AN INDEPENDENT ASSESSMENT
OF AGENCY BUDGET REQUESTS BY THE LEGISLATURE

Several features in the legislature's environment discourage the independent assessment of agency budgets. These include: (1) the numerous tasks of the legislators and their inability to give more than brief attention to certain responsibilities; (2) limitations on the members' own information about agency financial needs and the limited staff facilities available to the members; and (3) the

71

members' reluctance to accept agency budget requests at their face value.

1. The broad responsibilities of legislators

The responsibilities of legislators are broad in scope and lead them to dissipate their energies. Aside from reviewing the budget requests of administrative agencies, legislators must consider bills which authorize new government activities or changes in existing programs. They must also receive and accommodate constituents who wish assistance in dealing with administrative agencies. This service aspect of the legislators' job is not limited to helping constituents who want the patronage of government jobs or government contracts. Legislators assist citizens who are confused by the myriad of forms that must be completed to qualify for certain public services, and they make inquiries to satisfy constituents who are denied services after their first application. Legislators also spend much service time in behalf of local governments within their district. Congressmen arrange appointments for local officials with federal administrators, and often lend their physical presence to the meetings. At the state level, legislators introduce "local bills" into the legislature, testify in behalf of their community's needs, and steer the bills through committees. Where the state constitution requires heavy state involvement in the authorization of local government activities, the legislators are kept busy as delegates from the city hall and the county courthouse.

Along with their legislative and service responsibilities, the members of Congress and state legislatures must attend to their own political needs. They spend time on their own careers and the success of their party. Some electoral activity occurs as the service work described above. Whenever a legislator assists a constituent or a local government, he may count it as an investment in the voters' good will. Other duties are more directly linked with re-election. Speaking engagements and tours are not restricted to the short period of the campaign. Many legislators campaign on a continuing basis, looking for voters' affections or money to restock their campaign treasuries.

2. The quality of legislators' information

Few legislators have the breadth of knowledge or experience to be personally aware of events over the whole range of their responsibilities. As a result, they cannot be fully aware of the issues in budgeting or other matters. They usually serve a "generalist" function in the political system. It may be good that persons with a mixture of educational and occupational experiences are given the opportunity to review and supervise the activities of "specialists" in the administrative agencies. It is part of their "representative" function that the legislators are somewhat like the rest of us in not being intimately aware of the features of government programs. At the same time, however, representatives are limited in what they can do by not having a complete understanding of their decisions on matters of legislation or appropriation.

There are some opportunities for U.S. Congressmen to learn about the issues they encounter. The seniority system protects a member's seat on his committee, and allows him to accumulate information over the years that will inform his decisions. Senators and Representatives also have personal staff assistants who do much of the service work for the member's constituents, review important issues in legislation, and help with fund raising and campaigning. Moreover, each Committee has its own professional staff which gathers information for the members, conducts formal hearings, and writes the Committee's *Reports*. Congress also enjoys the services of the General Accounting Office. This is an arm of the legislature, and its head (the Comptroller General) reports to the presiding officers of each house. As its name implies, the GAO has financial responsibilities. It conducts independent reviews of agency spending practices, evaluates programs, and supervises the accounting and auditing procedures of the agencies. The operations of the GAO are extensive. In 1966, its own budget was $48 million, and it employed almost 4,400 persons.

The members of state legislatures are less well-equipped than Congressmen to supervise and control administrative operations. The picture is generally one of ill-informed legislators and sparse staff assistance. State legislatures are weakened by the lack of viable seniority systems. In many states even chairmen do not have continuing rights to their committee assignments. A 1950 study found that 76 percent of the chairmen in the Senate of Alabama, 50 percent in the Senates of Maryland and Kentucky, and 43 percent in Georgia had only one previous term of experience. In lower houses there is even less of a tendency for chairmen to be senior members. Fifty percent of the chairmen in Vermont, 44 percent in

New Hampshire, 100 percent in Alabama, 83 percent in Kentucky, and 43 percent in Montana, Tennessee and Nevada had no more than one previous term as legislators.[1]

The lack of a viable seniority system reflects the unattractive nature of state legislatures and the high turnover of their members. The prestige, salary, and perquisites of state legislators are markedly inferior to those of Congressmen. A turnover rate of 40 percent (much of it voluntary) is not unusual in some states,[2] so there is little on which to build a seniority system. Half of the states pay their legislators less than $4,000 per year and nine of the states pay less than $2,000.[3] The expense allowances and clerical and professional staffs of legislators are similarly inadequate. In several states, the legislators have no office or secretary of their own. Without a seniority system, state legislatures are unlikely to develop any financial expertise among their members. Where budget committees do not provide adequate staff assistance, a tenure and an opportunity for members to learn their jobs, they are likely to become highly dependent upon the recommendations of the chief executive.

State legislatures are restricted further by the decisions they are allowed to make. The constitutions of several states require that expenditures not exceed projected revenues. Some states also have additional restrictions. The legislatures of Maryland and West Virginia may reduce the funds that the governor recommends for any agency, but increase only those recommended for the legislature or (in West Virginia) the judiciary. In Nebraska, a simple majority may reduce the governor's recommendations but a three-fifths vote is necessary to increase them. In Rhode Island, any increases voted over the governor's recommendations must be covered by revenue estimates or existing surpluses, or by additional financing enacted along with the budget.[4] When these constraints are viewed along with the poor informational resources of the state legislatures, the members' plight appears even more difficult. They are weakened by a lack of formal prerogatives and weakened further by poor opportunities to base their decisions on sound information.

3. The legislators' distrust of agency requests

The legislators' reluctance to accept the agencies' budget requests at their face value reflects a distrust of administrators that has its roots in the constitutional separation of powers and checks and balances. The major ingredients of this system are a bicameral legislature, a separately-elected chief executive, and a judiciary that is independent of either the executive or the legislature. Each branch has certain tools to protect itself from encroachment by the others, and the officers of each are given a separate constituency or a separate method of selection in order to reinforce their suspicion of one another. In *Federalist #51,* James Madison defended this fractured structure as it would apply to the federal government. Insofar as state and local governments are—with few exceptions— modelled after the federal separation of powers-checks and balances, the same sentiments apply at lower levels of government.

. . . the great security against a gradual concentration of the several powers in the same department consists in giving to those who ad-minister each department the necessary constitutional means and personal motives to resist encroachment of others. . . . Ambition must be made to counteract ambition. . . . If men were angels, no govern-ment would be necessary. If angels were to govern men, neither external nor internal controls on government would be necessary. In framing a government which is to be administered by men over men, the great difficulty lies in this: you must first enable the government to control the governed; and in the next place oblige it to control itself.

The separation of powers and checks and balances were contrived to enable each branch of the government to control the others. As part of the latter-day manifestations of this intragovernmental an-tagonism, we find the legislature being unwilling to enact the agencies' budgets simply as they are submitted by the adminis-trators.

It is not solely on account of constitutional traditions that legislatures are inclined not to accept the agencies' budgets. Legis-latures tend to be financially conservative, while the agencies are expansive in making their budget requests. The administrators seek to stretch their programs by adding to their appropriations, partly because they equate an improved program with an increased budget. (See the discussion of the spending-service cliche in Chap-ter VI). In contrast, the legislators are among the hardest-working of the incrementalists. They seek to minimize the expenditures by holding down agency budget growth.[5]

THE ATTRACTIONS OF THE EXECUTIVE'S RECOMMENDATION

Despite their reluctance to accept the budget requests of admin-istrative agencies, legislators are unable to make a separate investigation of the agencies' needs. They are short on relevant training, experience, and staff assistance. They need outside help in order to evaluate the agencies' requests. Without some guidance, they might blunder into allowing an "extravagant" budget, or be overly severe in cutting funds below the level that is sufficient to maintain services at desirable levels. By and large, the legislators look to the chief executive as the source of budget recommendations. Although the executive as an individual suffers from some of the same lack of relevant training and experience as members of the legislature, he is likely to have more sophisticated staff assistance. The President has his Bureau of the Budget. This has an appropriation of about $8 million annually and a staff of 500. State governors have comparable facilities, although seldom as well-staffed as the U.S. Budget Bureau. These organizations review agency requests, and prepare for their budget decisions by a continuing assessment of agency programs. Professional budget analysts tend to work with the same agencies year after year, and they can acquire as much understanding of agency operations as is possible for an "outsider."

The legislative's reliance on the chief executive's budget recommendations is not a perfect solution. The chief executive is identified with the agencies as their chief administrative officer. There is tension between the legislature and the executive that reflects the traditional animosities associated with the separation of powers— checks and balances. However, the chief executive provides the only evaluation of agency budgets that is always available for every agency. Moreover, the chief executive's recommendations tend to be lower than the agency requests, and are therefore consistent with the legislature's desire for small increments of growth. Other assessments of agency budgets come from interest groups. However, interest groups comment only about the items that interest them, and they may be intense in their support of certain programs. Interest group recommendations frequently are more generous than even the agency's own request.[6]

CONGRESSIONAL RELIANCE ON THE PRESIDENT'S
BUDGET RECOMMENDATIONS

It is difficult to assess the operation of the legislator's acceptance of executive's budget cues in the federal government. There is no distinction made between the agencies' own requests for funds and the recommendation of the President. This distinction is hidden in order to prevent the agencies from seeking funds not desired as part of the President's program. Unfortunately for analysis, the lack of such distinction limits our testing the saliency of the administrators' or the President's request for the decisions of Congress.

Despite these problems, some studies of federal budgeting show a high correspondence between the recommendations of the President and the appropriations of Congress. Although we lack the opportunity to state whether the President's own recommendations or the initial requests of administrators are valued more highly by Congress, we can state that the funds typically voted by Congress bear a strong resemblance to those requested by the President. In the preceding chapter we described several decision rules which reveal the dependence of Congressmen on the information presented to them in the President's budget. The "agency's request" indicated in those rules is actually the recommendation of the Bureau of the Budget, in the name of the President. The rules show that Congress typically responds to the amount requested on behalf of the agency, or to the amount requested in the current year as it is "adjusted" by the congressmen's reassessment of their treatment of the agency during the previous year (see pp 52–53). Another study of Congressional budget-making has reported the percentage difference between the President's requests for several agencies during the 1947–62 period, and the appropriations voted in the House and Senate. Of 36 agencies studied, only seven of them received a sum from the House of Representatives that varied by an average of 10 percent from the President's recommendation. During the same period, only one of the 36 agencies received a sum from the Senate that varied from the President's recommendation by an average of 10 percent. These findings concentrate on the budgets of domestic agencies, and so may exaggerate the strength of congressional acceptance of the President's budget recommendations. They omit foreign-aid and military agencies, including the jurisdiction of such a notorious "budget cutter" as Representative Otto Passman. However, there is some other evidence that the Appropriations Committee attempts to minimize excessive budget cutting wherever it occurs. In 1965 Chairman Mahon sought to "liberalize" the subcommittee which was chaired by Representative Passman in order to balance program support against the subcommittee's proclivity for making sizable reductions in the executive's request.[7]

THE RELIANCE OF STATE LEGISLATURES ON THE GOVERNOR'S BUDGET RECOMMENDATIONS

The variety of political and economic conditions in the states provides an opportunity to examine many different manifestations of legislative reliance on the chief executive's budget cues. The findings come from the same study of agency-governor-legislature relationships in 19 states that was examined in Chapter IV. The focus here is upon the dependence of the legislators on the governor's recommendations. Because the raw material pertains to 19 different states and 592 separate agencies, it is possible to depict the general picture of the legislature's dependence on the governor, and conditions under which its dependence is greater or less than usual.

Both the governor and the legislature respond negatively in the short run to agency acquisitiveness. It is the size of the *increment* requested by each agency, rather than the size of the request, per se, which triggers the response of the governor and the legislature. Both seem to be using the same (incremental) decision rules. They cut the requests of agencies that ask for sizable increases, and they give no increase beyond those which the agencies request. Although both the governor and the legislature give similar treatment to agency requests, they do not employ similar procedures of evaluation. In most states the legislature accepts the governor's recommendations. When the governor recommends a cut in an agency budget, the legislature typically cuts approximately the amount that is recommended. A state legislature seldom makes independent assessment of budget requests.[8]

An intensive analysis of agency-governor-legislature relationships in Georgia during the 1965–66 biennium, shows that the executive's recommendation remains the most prominent influence on that legislature among several additional factors that were taken into account. These additional factors included the *number of agency employees* and the *number of program activities* listed in their budget request; the percentage of each agency's request that would be *financed with federal funds;* the percentage of each agency's request that would be *spent on personnel,* and the percentage to be *spent on capital facilities;* the *success of each agency's request in the previous session of the Legislature.* None of these additional factors were as important for the legislature's decisions as the recommendations of Governor Carl Sanders.[9]

The Georgia governor is so powerful in the eyes of the legislature that members have accepted his budget recommendations even when there was virtually no incumbent. The budget for fiscal 1968 was submitted by outgoing Governor Carl Sanders, whose term was supposed to have expired at the end of 1966. However, neither Republican candidate Howard Callaway nor the Democrat Lester Maddox had received a majority of the popular vote in November 1966, and they were awaiting the outcome of the legislature's selection of the next governor. Maddox was chosen by the legislature, but he had little opportunity to review Sanders' lame duck budget and make his own recommendations during the time the legislature was permitted to sit. Despite the "interregnum" quality of the executive's recommendations, however, there was an equally close correspondence between the executive's recommendations and the legislature's appropriations during that year as there was during each normal budget cycle during the 1963–69 period. The governor of Georgia has several formal and informal powers that lead the legislature to accept the executive's recommendations even when it must anticipate an incumbent in office. A number of these powers also characterize other southern chief executives.[10] Aside from wide-ranging powers of appointment, southern governors involve themselves in the selection of highways to be built or resurfaced, the choice of sites for the development of new state institutions, and the selection of existing institutions to be repaired or otherwise improved. Because southern state governments (including that of Georgia) support many services that are provided by local units in other sections of the country, the governor's power can go deeply into fields concerned with local schools, county roads, and the promotion of local industrial development.

DEVIATIONS FROM THE LEGISLATURE'S BUDGET ROUTINE

Even though the executive's recommendation is generally the most important consideration in the legislature's handling of agency budgets, this is not always the case. At the federal level, Congress has shown the sharpest deviations from customary budget practices during periods of political change. In 1948 the Republicans in control of the 80th Congress made a concerted effort to reduce President Truman's recommendations. In 1953–55 and 1962–63 there was no party conflict between the White House and Congress, but there was an unusually high frequency of deviations from normal budgeting. In 1953–55 the Republicans had control of both Congress and the Presidency for the first time in 20 years, and the Democrats were in a comparable position during the early 1960s. Perhaps in an effort to depart from past practices and realize their own policy goals, both the Republicans in 1953-55 and the Democrats in 1962–63 generated an unusually high incidence of executive-legislative conflict.[11] Also, the prominence of the legislature's acceptance of the executive's budget recommendations does not prevent individual congressmen from making themselves the nemisis of executives. Several Congressional budget cutters are on the minds of administrators and executives when they formulate their budget proposals. In this way, some legislators may influence executive budget decisions even before the document is presented to the legislature. Yet once the executive's budget is presented, it tends to dominate the legislature's actions.

Among the 19 states whose budget processes have been examined, there is considerable variation in the relationships between the governor's recommendation and the legislature's appropriation. Some legislatures are generally more disposed than others to accept the governor's recommendation. In each state, the governor's recommendation appears to be more (or less) important for the legislature's treatment of certain agencies than it is for others.

The legislature's reliance on the governor's budget tends to be *less than normal* where the governor has only limited tenure potential, where there is a high incidence of separately elected executive officials, and where total expenditures are relatively low.[12] Where the governor has only a limited opportunity to succeed himself in office, he may be limited in eliciting cooperation from the law-makers. Where there are many separately elected executives, they may present the governor with competition for the legislature's attention. And where expenditures are relatively low, legislators may be tempted to reject the governor's recommended budget cuts.

One study has shown that the legislatures of South Dakota,

Virginia, and Texas have made independent assessments of agency budget requests.[13] The constitutions and statutes of these states include formal provisions which may assist the legislature in making its budget inquiries. Their budget regulations provide for an early submission of agency requests to the legislature (within five days of convening); and the legislature of each state has unlimited discretion in altering the agency budgets. In contrast to the discretion of these legislatures, some other legislatures can only increase the governor's recommendations under certain (difficult) conditions. And some legislatures must wait up to six weeks into the session before they receive the governor's recommendations.[14]

In 1965 the Nebraska Legislature acted consistently in opposition to the recommendations of Governor Frank B. Morrison. Where he recommended severe budget cuts the legislature gave favorable treatment to the agency. This conflict was part of a more basic antagonism between the Democratic governor and the Republican legislature. Their enmity was particularly intense in the area of tax legislation, where the principal issue was a proposal for a broad-based state tax. At the time, Nebraska was almost alone among the states in its reliance on the property tax to the exclusion of either a state sales tax or a state income tax. Observers in Nebraska report that legislators sought to force a new tax on the Governor by rejecting his recommendations for reductions in agency budget requests.

The administration of Governor John Reynolds of Wisconsin (1963–65) provides another example of weak rapport between the governor and the legislature on budget matters.[15] Governor Reynolds was known for his social commitment, and for the intensity of his conflicts with a legislature that was both more conservative than he, and controlled by members of the opposition party. The scope of Reynold's conflict with the legislature ranged over a wide spectrum of issues that included tax policy and the confirmation of his appointees, as well as budgeting. As a budget-maker, Reynolds was virtually unique among governors in accepting the requests of even the most expansionist agencies. He transmitted their requests for large increments virtually intact to the hostile legislature, which proceeded to make a separate evaluation of agency requests. Some participants in that budget process accuse the governor of being naive in his support of agencies that customarily padded their budgets in anticipation of reductions. According to one report, an agency spokesman actually asked for cuts in the legislature because his unit could not spend its entire request in one fiscal period.

By examining the budget records of *individual agencies*, it is possible to identify other features associated with the legislature's lack of reliance on the governor's budget recommendations. State colleges and universities show a high incidence of appropriations that are markedly above or below the level of the governor's recommendations. This suggests that state colleges and universities are among the most controversial of government agencies. Higher education consumes a larger percentage of state budgets than any function except highways, and constituents appear to be unusually interested in measures pertaining to colleges and universities. Budget decisions for higher education are charged with political excitement, and different groups may gain access to the governor and to the legislature. As a result, the legislature may be unable to accept the governor's budget recommendations.

Agencies in the economic development field also show a high incidence of both positive and negative deviations. Their budgets may be as controversial as those of colleges and universities, but for different reasons. Economic development is a popular, but elusive phenomenon whose attainment cannot be guaranteed by agency supporters. These agencies spend large sums on promotional activities, and occasionally they are subject to embarrassing exposures of unwise or extravagant campaigns. The promise of economic growth may lead some legislatures to be more generous than the governor with these agencies, while disappointments in their results or a lack of confidence in their programs may lead other legislatures to be unusually stingy.[16]

A study of agency budgets in Wisconsin over the 1957–67 period revealed that agencies in the fields of taxation, law enforcement, and economic regulation tend to receive appropriations that were *lower* than predicted on the basis of the governors' recommendations. These findings are consistent with other observations about the fate of agencies charged with unpleasant duties: they suffer from the complaints of individuals and groups whose activities are curtailed by agency efforts, and those who complain are frequently important in the economy and politics.[17]

SUMMARY AND CONCLUSION

The legislators' reliance on the budget recommendations of the chief executive shows some elements of the incremental routine that is considered in Chapter IV. Legislators begin their calculations from the decisions made by the actor immediately prior to themselves in the budget process: the chief executive. The legislatures' decision typically varies only incrementally from the executive's budget. However, the stimuli that lead legislators to rely on the executive's budget recommendations are not entirely the same as those which underlie incrementalism. By distinguishing the two routines, it is possible to identify special features in the legislative-executive relationship, and add another dimension to the understanding of decision-making routines in the budget process. The foundation of the legislature's reliance on the executive's budget recommendation seems to lie in the relative weaknesses of the legislature, and in a relative strength of the chief executive. In truth, both institutions show certain weaknesses in their relationships with administrative agencies. The personnel in both dissipate investigatory and creative energies on the many features of government and politics that are forced on them by their jobs. The governor and legislators are usually unprepared for their responsibilities by either systematic training or prior occupational experience. As individuals, neither the legislators nor the chief executive have the resources to comprehend the full range of administrative programs that come before them in periodic budget requests. However, the chief executive possesses institutional strengths in the form of staff expertise. In effect, his recommendations are those of professional analysts in the central budget office. At the national level this is the Bureau of the Budget. At the state level it is a similar institution that may carry a variety of labels.[18] At either level, the central budget office provides to the chief executive a degree of expertise that exceeds any that is available to the legislature. As a result, the executive's recommendations provide the most well-informed advice that is consistently available about every agency. Legislators feel that they need help in reviewing agency budgets. In most cases, the executive's budget is the best assistance available.

Although the legislature's reliance on the executive's budget is the general tendency, this reliance is not universal. At the national level, the routine seems strongest after the upsets associated with major political changes have subsided, and where the executive and legislature have established "normal" relations. In the states, the routine is strongest where the governor can succeed himself in office, and where there is a low incidence of separately-elected administrators. The legislature seems most inclined to accede to the governor's recommendations where state expenditures are already high. Legislatures have ignored the routine for agencies in the fields of higher education, economic development, taxation, law enforcement, and economic regulation. And individual governors have embroiled themselves in severe conflicts with legislatures over matters that are outside the budget field, and thereby endangered their recommendations about expenditures.

NOTES

1. G. Theodore Mitau, *State and Local Government: Politics and Processes* (New York: Charles Scribner, 1966), p. 62.

2. Malcolm E. Jewell and Samuel C. Patterson, *The Legislative Process in the United States* (New York: Random House, 1966), p. 120.

3. John G. Grumm and Calvin W. Clark, *Compensation for Legislators in the Fifty States* (Kansas City, Missouri: Citizens Conference on State Legislators, 1966).

4. *Book of the States, 1964–65* (Chicago: Council of State Governments, 1964), pp. 159–67.

5. Aaron Wildavsky, *The Politics of the Budgetary Process* (Boston: Little, Brown, 1964), pp. 47 ff.

6. See my "Four Agencies and An Appropriations Subcommittee: A Comparative Study of Budget Strategies," *Midwest Journal of Political Science, IX* (August 1965), pp. 254–81.

7. Richard Fenno, *The Power of the Purse: Appropriations Politics in Congress* (Boston: Little, Brown, 1966), pp. 146, 368, 585.

8. See my "Agency Requests, Gubernatorial Recommendations, and Budget Success in State Legislatures," *American Political Science Review, LXII* (December 1968).

9. Ira Sharkansky and Augustus B. Turnbull III, "Budget Sucess in a State Legislature," 1968, mimeo.

10. Robert Highsaw, "The Southern Governor: Challenge to the Strong Governor Theme," *Public Administration Review,* 19 (1959), pp. 7–11.

11. Otto Davis, M. A. H. Dempster, Aaron Wildavsky, "A Theory of the Budgetary Press, *"American Political Science Review LX* (September 1966), pp. 529–47.

12. See my article cited in note 8.

13. See may article cited in note 8.

14. *Book of the States, 1964–65, op. cit.,* pp. 44–45, 159–67.

15. See Ira Sharkansky and Augustus B. Turnbull III, "Budget-Making in Georgia and Wisconsin: A Test of a Model," *Midwest Journal of Political Science, XIII* (November, 1969).

16. *Ibid.,* plus my *The Politics of Taxing and Spending* (Indianapolis: Bobbs-Merrill, 1969), Chapter IV.

17. See the articles cited in notes 8 and 15, plus Murray Edelman, *The Symbolic User of Politics* (Urbana: University of Illinois Press, 1967), Chapter 2.

18. The titles of the governor's chief budget officer include Finance Director, Budget Director, Comptroller, Commisioner of Administration.

VI. Regional Consultation: Copy Your Neighbor[1]

INCREMENTAL BUDGETING AND LEGISLATORS' RELIANCE ON THE executive's budget recommendations are routines that guide officials to take their decision-cues from within their own governmental system. The routine of incremental budgeting uses earlier expenditure decisions as points of departure in budget-making for the coming period. The routine legislative action in dealing with budget requests is to accept the executive's recommendation as the principal point of departure. This chapter deals with a routine which guides the officials of state and local governments when they look outside their own jurisdictions for new ideas. Decision cues do not come invariably from inside one's own government. When government officials look outside of their own organizations, they tend not to search the entire country to find the "one best model." They simplify their task by generally looking first to regional neighbors.

FEATURES SUPPORTING REGIONAL CONSULTATIONS AMONG PUBLIC OFFICIALS

Several features support the routine of regional consultation. These include (1) the officials' belief that neighbors have problems similar to their own; (2) the attitude of officials and interested citizens that it is "legitimate" to adapt one's own programs to those of nearby governments; and (3) the structure of organizational affiliations which put officials into frequent contact with their counterparts in neighboring governments.

1. Similarities in conditions

Many government officials believe that neighboring jurisdictions have problems similar to their own. Because neighboring governments serve similar populations, it is likely that the people have common needs for public service, and present similar demands to government agencies. The economies of the neighboring governments are generally alike, and they present a comparable set of resources and needs to government agencies. And the political environment is likely to be similar in neighboring jurisdictions; politicians will probably support comparable levels of service, and there may be similar relationships between administrators, the executive and the legislature. The resemblances between neighboring jurisdictions in their population, economic, and political characteristics may be the results of underlying geographical and historical similarities. Shared traits of geography may lead to similar economic and population characteristics, and shared historical experiences may give rise to common political values and similar desires for public services.

The state governments in the South are commonly perceived to represent the archetype of American regions. They share certain geographical features that have affected politics through the intermediary of the cotton-plantation-slave syndrome. They also shared historical experiences of racial heterogeneity, Civil War, Reconstruction, continuing poverty, and limited political participation and competition. Many government services in the South are distinctive but the South is not the only distinctive region. States in the Great Lake and Rocky Mountain areas, in particular, share traits that seem to reflect common features of population, geography, history, economics, and politics.

2. The legitimacy of regionalism

The routines of regional consultation is considered "legitimate" because many political actors in each state believe that similar conditions may be found throughout the region. It is felt that neighbors face similar problems with similar resources, so the norms which guide their service decisions are likely to be within reach of one's own government agencies. Thus, the adaptation to regional models is considered "relevant," "easy," or "feasible" in the light of local conditions. For officials in Georgia, it is "reasonable" (i.e., legitimate) to adopt patterns that are found in Florida, North Carolina, or Tennessee; but the programs found in New York, Michigan, or California have been called "out of reach," "impractical," or "designed for a different set of needs." Politicians, journalists, and members of the public who take an interest in certain programs are accustomed to comparing efforts within

their own state to those which are in their own circle of experience, and this circle typically is limited to the region. State
bureaus of research usually publish comparisons of their own
state's demographic, economic, and public service characteristics
with those of regional partners. This information provides additional fuel and status to the comparison of one's own efforts with
those of the neighborhood. In the *Georgia Statistical Abstract,* for
example (published by the University's Bureau of Business and
Economic Research), data for the state as a whole is compared
with a figure for the entire United States, and with separate
figures for Alabama, Florida, North Carolina, South Carolina,
and Tennessee. When a study committee of the University of
Wisconsin analyzed tax burdens in that state, the comparisons
were drawn with Illinois, Indiana, Iowa, Michigan, Minnesota,
and Ohio.[2]

The legitimacy of regional comparisons tends to feed upon past
habit. Because officials have consulted with their counterparts in
nearby governments, they have learned who can be trusted for
credible information, candor, and good judgment. Unless an
official is committed to an extensive program of research before
making his own policy decisions, he may be satisfied after making
a few calls to individuals with whom he has dealt amicably in the
past.

3. Regional associations

The professional activities of government officials also lead
them to regional neighbors for policy cues. Policy-makers and
professional employees of state and local governments belong to
formal organizations according to their subject matter specialty.
There are now at least 46 of these groups.[3] They include the
National Association of State Budget Officers, the National Association of State Conservation Officers, and the National Association of Housing and Redevelopment Officials. They have both
national and regional meetings that provide the opportunity for
trading information about current problems and reinforcing
friendships that had been formed at earlier meetings. State and
local officials indicate that they are more likely to attend the
regional than the national meetings of these groups, and they
acquire many of their contacts at these meetings.

Federal agencies which distribute grants-in-aid to state and local units played a part in the establishment of some regional associations for government officials. Federal officers use them as informal communications media that supplement their formal contacts with state and local agencies. Federal grants for some programs include agency dues to these professional associations, so the federal government provides a continuing subsidy to keep them in operation. Federal agencies also encourage regional communications by virtue of their field offices. The cities of New York, Atlanta, Chicago, Dallas, Kansas City, Denver, and San Francisco have acquired informal status as regional capitals because they contain the offices of numerous Washington agencies. The personnel in these field offices conduct most of the correspondence between the federal agency and state and local units, and they help to pass the news of problems and solutions from one state government to another within their regions.

REGIONAL PATTERNS OF INTERGOVERNMENTAL COMMUNICATION

There is a paucity of solid evidence about the political intercourse between officials of different state and local governments. On a questionnaire that was administered to the budget officers of 67 major agencies[4] in the states of Florida, Georgia, Kentucky, and Mississippi, one question asked: *Have you or any of your colleagues contracted officials in other states in an attempt to learn how they deal with a particular situation that you have encountered in your work?* Where a budget officer answered in the affirmative he was asked: *What states do you feel are the best sources of information?* The 67 respondents made 198 nominations of states that were among the "best sources of information." Most (87 percent) of their nominations were in the region that includes the eleven states of the Confederacy and the Border States of Delaware, Maryland, Kentucky, West Virginia, and Oklahoma. Thirty-five percent of the nominations were states that bordered directly on the respondents'. Although it is conceivable that Southerners are more parochial in their reliance on neighbors than officials in other sections of the country, officials elsewhere likewise refer primarily to states in the immediate or near neighborhood when questioned about the source of their own policy norms.

A survey conducted among school superintendents in Georgia illuminates the regional orientation of these local government officers. A sample of 20 superintendents[5] were asked to identify which officials they contacted when they felt the need to discuss a local problem with an outside expert. The results show a strong tendency to contact the superintendents who are immediate neighbors, or who are fellow members of one's administrative region. In Georgia, these administrative regions are coterminous with the Congressional Districts. The State Department of Education plans its activities on a District basis and superintendents in each District have periodic meetings.

The superintendents made 36 nominations of frequent outside contacts. Forty-two percent of these were superintendents within their own administrative region; and 70 percent were either contiguous, within their administrative region, or within a common metropolitan area. The responses suggest that the choice of a contact is an uncomplicated one, guided by a notion of friends and neighbors within easy reach. One rural superintendent described his daily route as the guide to contacts: "Well, I live in Macon County, so I have to drive (to work) through Marion and Schley Counties. I talk with those there pretty often." Several of the superintendents administer relatively large, urban districts. But only one of these stood apart from the prevailing regional orientation in selecting his contacts. The superintendent of Chatham County (Savannah) said that he sought advice from his counterparts in other large districts throughout the state.

Although it seems that government officials are inclined to look within their region for policy cues, the questions remains: *Which regional partners are the targets of emulation?* From the comments of several officials, it is evident that governments which have acquired a reputation for leadership are sought out disproportionately for their advice. There may be separate routines in jurisdictions which are leaders and followers in each region. Most government officials seem inclined to copy the leading agencies within their region. The leading agencies either generate their own innovations, or take their cues from other leaders outside their immediate region. Professor Jack L. Walker of the University of Michigan has gathered evidence on the timing of innovations in each of the 48 contiguous states. By aggregating data across several fields of service he ranked the state governments according to their adoption of programs or policies earlier—or later—than other states. His rankings suggest that New York and

Massachusetts play leadership roles in the Northeast, Michigan and Wisconsin in the middle section of the country, California on the West Coast, Colorado in the Mountain region, and Louisiana and Virginia in the South.[6]

The ambiguous regional location of some states provides their officials with special opportunities to specify their regional routine. Where a state is situated on the borders between different regions, its officials can choose among several states as the subject of comparison. When they face a situation where they must plead for additional funds, they can identify themselves as the poor cousin in comparison with more well-endowed neighbors. But when they find it necessary to defend themselves against public criticism they can picture themselves as offering better services than other neighbors. Educators in Missouri, for example, often find it necessary to justify their low level of expenditure for public schools. In 1959, the state ranked 38th in per capita expenditures for local schools, but 18th in per capita income. When they are on the defensive, Missouri officials can compare their efforts to the low-ranking neighbors of Arkansas, Oklahoma, and Nebraska, rather than to high-ranking Illinois.[7]

REGIONAL PATTERNS OF PUBLIC POLICY

We must be cautious in accepting regional patterns of public policy as evidence of the copy-your-neighbor routine. State and local governments in various regions might come to similar types and levels of policy because of experiences other than the regional consultations of government officials. *Levels of economic development* affect the needs of populations and the resources available to governments, and they have a powerful influence on the nature of services that are provided.[8] Because regional partners tend to resemble one another economically, these economic traits may produce similar levels of revenues, expenditures, and public services. In order to eliminate regional patterns that are likely to be the product of economic affinities, we shall control our findings for three aspects of economic development: personal welfare, urbanization, and total economic resources.[9]

By examining some distinctive regional policies that are not simply a product of current economic conditions, we shall gain some insight into the variety of factors which seem to have contributed to regional norms. The data of Table VI-1 show the

TABLE VI-1

Ratios between Actual Policy Scores and those Scores Predicted on the Basis of Three Economic Characteristics

	New Eng.	Mid. Atl.	South East	Great Lakes	Plains	Mount.	South West	Far West
1) total state expend./capita	.941	.956	.972	.889	.876	1.659*	1.152*	1.287*
2) state educ. expend./capita	.583*	.855	.924	.741*	.762*	1.128	1.171*	1.279*
3) state highw. expend./capita	1.109	.747*	.864	.976	.938	1.473*	1.168*	1.081
4) state pub. welf. expend./capita	1.053	.778*	.977	.822*	1.011	.978	1.152*	1.336
5) total state and local expend./capita	.960	.874	.915	.927	.985	1.162*	1.050	1.131
6) s+1 educ. expend./capita	.847*	.854	.860	.964	1.109	1.217*	1.111	1.136
7) s+1 highw. expend./capita	.994	.657*	.761	.809*	.957	1.227*	1.006	.902
8) s+1 pub. welf. expend./capita	1.064	.755*	.917	.854	1.053	1.022	1.059	1.141
9) state taxes/personal income	.893	1.036	1.034	.875	.807*	.978	1.087	1.239*
10) state and local tax/personal income	1.049	.952	.938	.984	1.032	1.110	1.028	1.062
11) property tax collections/capita	1.116	.769*	.686	1.041	1.150*	1.138	.814*	.825*
12) sales tax/capita	.623*	.644*	1.168*	1.181*	.860	.883	.997	1.817*
13) excise tax/capita	1.082	1.012	1.089	.849*	.832	.866	.867	1.127
14) motor veh. tax/capita	.872	.852	.716*	1.084	1.106	1.288*	1.486*	1.201*
15) income tax/capita	.766*	1.711*	.970	.505*	.784*	1.522*	1.056	.823*
16) current charges/capita	.694*	.941	.990	.939	1.021	1.115	1.217*	1.217*
17) debt/capita	1.039	1.218*	1.176*	.818*	.834*	.813*	.994	1.889
18) percent state and local rev. to state	1.092	1.075	1.016	.858	.888	.993	1.136	1.100
19) percent rev. from non-local sources	1.082	.921	.919	1.089	1.216*	1.021	.854	.856
20) fed. aid as a percent of s+1 revenue	1.004	.825*	.956	.826*	.890	1.232*	1.084	1.255*
21) percent enrollment using school lunch program	.861	1.019	1.074	.894	1.087	.988	.879	.959
22) enrollment in vocat. educ./10,000 pop.	.628*	.733*	1.111	.849*	.967	1.035	1.005	1.641*
23) enrollment in vocational rehab./10,000 pop.	1.061	1.175*	1.146	.712*	.924	.957	.798*	.709*

TABLE VI-1 (continued)

	New Eng.	Mid. Atl.	South East	Great Lakes	Plains	Mount.	South West	Far West
24) persons completing vocational rehab./10,000 pop.	1.034	1.930*	1.366*	.810*	.754*	.938	.739*	.838*
25) percent graduating from high school	.931	.948	.891	1.092	1.146	1.076	.983	1.011
26) percent passing selective service mental exam.	.977	.837*	.813	.983	1.101	1.153*	1.043	.961
27) total road mileage/capita	.726*	.872*	1.063	.479*	.770*	1.435*	1.696*	1.327*
28) rural road mileage/rural resident	.300*	.346*	.588*	.741*	1.224*	1.994*	2.126*	1.613*
29) urban road mileage/urban resident	.777*	.522*	.818*	.821*	1.322*	1.067	1.186*	.851
30) percent I system open by 1962	1.121	.889	.778*	1.139	1.037	.809*	1.273*	1.005
31) percent farms on paved roads	1.117	.951	.951	1.134	1.068	.961	.784*	.974
32) population per road death	1.435*	1.134	1.041	.953	.978	.748*	.685*	.703*
33) AFDC payment/recipient	1.089	.912	.810*	1.063	1.106	1.175*	1.042	.932
34) OAA payment/recipient	1.014	.889	.877	1.036	1.478*	1.054	1.030	1.045
35) AB payment/recipient	1.118	.822*	.910	.986	1.101	1.002	1.105	1.090
36) APTD payment/recipient	1.232*	.938	.822*	1.165*	1.124	.998	1.071	.765*
37) AFDC recipients/persons w. incomes below $2,000	.975	1.102	1.085	.809*	.691*	1.114	1.033	1.191*
38) OAA recipients/persons over 65/ incomes below $2,000	.563*	.310*	1.1976	.248*	.485*	1.762*	1.828*	2.160*
39) AB recipients/ personal incomes below $2,000	.885	1.909*	1.234*	1.001	.882	.792*	1.392*	1.828*
40) APTD recipients/persons of incomes below $2,000	.953	.890	.991	.688*	.662*	1.589*	.673*	1.757*

For a more complete report of ratios for additional regional groupings, see my *Regionalism in American Politics* (Indianapolis: Bobbs-Merrill, 1969).

*ratios removed from 1.00 by at least .15.

extent to which a regional trait differs from that commonly associated with its level of economic development. Figures below 1.00
show a lower score on a trait than expected on the basis of the
region's economy. Figures above 1.00 show a higher score on a
trait than expected on the basis of the region's economy.[10] The data
pertain to 1962, and show the level of state and local government
activities with respect to government spending, taxation, the receipt
of federal and state financial aids by state and local governments,
and levels of public services in the fields of education, highways,
and welfare.

New England

New England shows several policy characteristics that are different from the expectations associated with its economy. Spending
for education and service levels in vocational education are lower
than expected; road systems are less-well developed; there is less
use of the major taxes collected by state governments (retail sales
and individual income); and slightly more use of the locally-
collected property tax than expected. Although a sales tax enacted by Massachusetts in 1966 will help to align that state's revenue
structure to the national norm, the long struggle preceding the
legislature's approval indicated severe resistance to the innovation. As late as 1962 state and local governments in Massachusetts received 53 percent of their tax revenue from property tax,
while governments throughout the country drew only 30 percent
of their tax revenue from this source. The tax structure in the
New England states reflects localistic norms that have prevailed
since colonial times. Unlike the colonies further south, those in
New England developed a number of viable, quasi independent
towns and cities. In part this reflected the relative density of
settlement in the northern colonies, and it drew some impetus
from the religious orientation of the settlers. The colonists were
Congregationalists, whose concern for local autonomy extended to
government as well as religion.

The prominence of private schools in New England works
against the region's expenditures for public education and its use
of one federal program (for vocational education) that is not
generally available to private school pupils. The heavy use of
private education reflects a combination of elite Yankee schools

and Roman Catholic parochial schools. Now the incidence of Roman Catholic parochial education far outweighs the older traditions represented by Groton, Andover, Exeter, and Saint Marks. In the heavily Catholic states of Rhode Island and Massachusetts, 29.4 and 23.6 percent of the elementary and secondary school pupils attend non-public institutions. In the field of higher education, the status and facilities of Harvard, Massachusetts Institute of Technology, Yale, Brown, and Dartmouth have long stood above the major public institutions in their states. As late as 1964, tiny Amherst College (1,100 students) reported more volumes in its library than the University of Massachusetts (8,500 students). The private school emphasis occasionally figures in the politics of New England. Supporters of parochial schools argue that public authorities shirk their obligations to support the thousands of students in private schools, while spokesmen for public education feel that opposition from private school parents subverts their own budgetary efforts for public schools.

In scoring lower than expected on both rural and municipal road mileage, the New England region typifies the low ratio of roads to population that is found in all of the older and more congested sections. Perhaps a combination of deterring costs of new construction, the efficiency of road mileage in congested areas, and a limited concern for highways is the explanation for "underdeveloped" road networks. Each mile of new road is likely to upset existing landowners; urban roads carry lots of vehicles more efficiently than roads in rural areas; and the relatively short distances between population centers may accustom drivers to the problems of heavy traffic and reduce their demands for more roads.[11] New England's favorable score on the road safety measure suggests that people do relatively little driving in congested areas.

Middle Atlantic

The distinctive traits of the Middle Atlantic region include lower spending and lower mileage in the highway field than expected on the basis of economic traits, plus low scores on a measure of educational service (examination success), low reliance on property and sales taxation, and high reliance on income taxation and government borrowing. The low spending and mileage figures for highways in the Middle Atlantic region reflect conditions similar to those in neighboring New England. The relatively low score examination success may reflect the continuing influx of migrants to the large cities of New York, New Jersey, Pennsylvania, and Maryland, and a resulting high level of cultural dissonance. Although measures of economic development generally show close relationship with measures of educational success, the enormous wealth of the Middle Atlantic region may deter high scores on this trait. Historically the region's wealth has attracted poor Europeans and more recently migrants from the rural South and the Caribbean; the urban ghettoes affect low scores on educational attainment at the same time that they indicate economic vitality in their surroundings.

The high reliance on government borrowing in the Middle Atlantic region may reflect the tax crises that two of its states experienced in recent years. Both New York and New Jersey have now enacted state-wide general sales taxes, but these innovations were sharp departures from political tradition, and came only after protracted executive-legislative struggles. Because existing tax structures could not produce revenues to meet service demands, and because members of the executive and legislature could not agree on an easier solution to revenue needs, the opportunities for borrowing may have looked especially tempting. In the case of New York the traditional tax of reliance was a relatively progressive individual income tax. As late as 1962, state and local governments in New York received 19 percent of their revenue from such a tax while the national average was 7 percent. In the case of New Jersey the tradition was to avoid broad-based state taxes. Until 1966 the state was one of two hold-outs (with Nebraska) against either an income or sales tax. State tax funds were so sparse in New Jersey during the early 1960s that Rutgers University built new classrooms on the ground floors of student dormitories. The students helped to pay for these classrooms with their room fees.

Great Lakes

The distinctive traits of the Great Lakes region have been lower scores than expected on income taxation and government indebtedness. For the immediate explanation of these traits, we need look no further than state constitutions. Those of Michigan and Illinois prohibit "progressive" personal income taxes, and those of Indiana, Michigan, Ohio, and Wisconsin put severe restrictions upon government borrowing. Although the Lake states evade their own constitutional limitations against debt by allowing public corporations to issue "non-guaranteed" bonds (e.g., for college dormitories and toll roads),[12] these restrictions against borrowing may hold down total indebtedness. The debt limits appeared in the state constitutions of the region during the nineteenth century, partly in response to a rash of defaulted bond issues that had been used to support turnpikes, railroads, and canals. Because of their over-extended obligations, midwestern politicians wrote fiscal conservatism into their state constitutions, and it became part of the region's policies.

Mountain

Despite a reputation for conservatism, state and local governments of the Mountain region show among the highest scores (relative to economic features) on measures of spending, federal aid, and the outputs of public service. An unusually large amount of the land area in the Mountain region is held by the federal government, and western Congressmen have won acceptance of the principal that Washington should give additional support to states with large acreage in the public domain. Upwards of 30 percent of the land in each Mountain state is owned by federal agencies, and this factor earns special recognition in the allocation formulae of several grant-in-aid programs.

Relative to economic conditions, state and local government expenditures in the Mountain region are the highest of any region in the country. The region also ranks at or near the top on the measures of road mileage, the success of residents on a national educational examination, the generosity of welfare payments for families of dependent children, and the recipient rates for Old Age Assistance and Aid to the Permanently and Totally Disabled. These traits add up to a cultural bias in favor of community-mindedness that stands in odd contrast to the success that right-wing Republicans have recently enjoyed in Montana, Wyoming, and Idaho. Several ingredients of the region's history may shed some light on the "progressive" norms of public services: the

radical labor movements that developed in the late 19th and early
20th century out of the hardships in mining and lumber camps;
the great distances, severe terrain, and isolation of population
settlements that might enforce a certain amount of cooperation
(at the same time that they provide a rationale for extreme
individualism); and the absence of large cultural minorities whose
extreme poverty or distinctiveness might have discouraged the
dominant population groups from accepting heavy tax levies.
Thus, the cultural homogeneity, the severity of the environment,
and the reaction to earlier excesses of a free enterprise economy
may have combined to mold the distinct character of policies in
the Mountain region.

Western Highways

A combination of traits that appears generally throughout the
western regions (Southwest, Mountain, Far West) includes highway mileage and motor vehicle taxes considerably higher than
expected on the basis of economic characteristics, and road safety
scores that are considerably below expectations. The impression
given by these figures is a section that is heavily dependent upon
automobile and truck transportation. Perhaps the great distance
between population centers is at the heart of this highway orientation. People live far apart from one another and require relatively
high investments in road mileage relative to population. In the
Mountain states the terrain makes these miles difficult and costly
to construct. Because it is customary to make the users pay for
highways, the heavy expenditures for roads require high gasoline
taxes. The orientation toward road travel may also translate itself
into the high scores on automobile fatalities.

Southeast

The Southeastern states show a number of traits that are
claimed for them by political scientists and historians, even after
controlling for their low levels of personal well-being, urbanization, and total economic resources. They score significantly lower
than expected on the provision of services in the fields of education, highways, and public welfare, and they have high scores on
sales taxation.

The low levels of political participation and party competition may retard service levels in the South, and bring about regressive tax policies. With little public involvement or competition among elected officials, southern policy-makers have little incentive to liberalize their programs. The South's performance in the program to aid families of dependent children is especially poor and reflects AFDC's reputation for being a "Negroes' program." Similarly, the low regional scores on examination success reflect the cultural distance between southern Negroes and the dominant American society, and the failure of southern school systems to close the gap since Emancipation. The only service areas where the South scores high (relative to economic status) are in three educational programs that receive much of their support from the federal government and threaten the *least* disruptions in the social system: school lunches, vocational education, and vocational rehabilitation.

The regressive nature of southern revenue systems is apparent in the relatively high use of sales and excise taxes. Part of the explanation for the southern revenue pattern can be found in the extreme poverty of the area. The sales tax wins support partly because it is collected in tolerably small portions. Indeed, Mississippi pioneered in the development of the retail sales tax during the Depression when it sold tokens and collected mil taxes on the very smallest sales. Yet there is also a racial ingredient in the South's reliance on the sales tax. More than one state official in the region told me they favored the levy on retail sales because it "makes the niggers pay their share."

THE STRENGTH OF REGIONALISM IN THE FACE OF
NATIONALIZING PRESSURES

It is often alleged that distinct regional traits are disappearing in the face of several pressures for national uniformity.[13] These pressures include developments in transportation and communication that facilitate the nation-wide transmission of new products and techniques; and the increasing number and generosity of federal grants-in-aid that provide funds and program standards to state and local agencies. Some manifestations of national uniformity outside the sphere of governmental activities include the prominence of network programming on television, the absorption of locally-owned newspapers by national chains, the merger of locally-owned industries into corporate giants, the development of national labor markets for many professions and skilled trades, and the growing homogeneity of working conditions and consumer goods across the country. If these economic changes affect changes in the routines of government officials in regions that were formerly more isolated, then the nationalization of the economy may help to produce nationwide similarities in the policies of state and local governments.

Despite the elements that favor the development of nation-wide similarities in public policy, it is evident that regional patterns have not succumbed. The routine of regional consultation is evident in the peculiar traits of several regions in government spending, and levels of public service in the fields of education, highways and welfare, in the nature of state and local revenue systems, and in the use of intergovernmental revenues. The question remains, however, about *changes in regional patterns*. In this section we examine changes in regional policy. Because of limitations in the data that is available, we must forego an analysis of change for most of the policies that are considered above. Our focus must concentrate on changes in government spending over the 1902–62 period. Although the findings cannot encompass the whole range of policies that may be responding to pressures for nation-wide uniformity, they do point to an important qualification in the thesis of national homogeneity.

State and local governments across the country are becoming more alike in their levels of total spending per capita. This finding appears in Table VI-2, which shows coefficients of variability for each of five years since 1902. These statistics represent a standard deviation divided by a mean, and thereby indicate the degree of dispersion in a measure around the average. The coefficients of variability have grown smaller over time, thus indicating that states across the nation are becoming less dispersed—and therefore more alike—in their levels of total spending. At the same time, however, it is also apparent that the members of individual regions are becoming more alike in their levels of spending. Coefficients for the regions as well as the nation have generally decreased in size.

The growing national similarity in government spending is largely a reflection of developments in the Southeast. The states

TABLE VI-2

Changes in Regional and National Uniformity: Coefficients of Variability 1902–62 for Total State plus Local Government Spending per Capita

	U.S.	New Eng.	Mid. Atl.	South East	Great Lakes	Plains	Mountains	South West	Far West
1962	.192	.119	.140	.141	.094	.121	.189	.129	.095
1957	.219	.181	.146	.219	.091	.121	.148	.135	.137
1942	.292	.097	.207	.253	.077	.149	.070	.217	.082
1932	.378	.329	.275	.226	.152	.128	.204	.333	.268
1902	.672	.367	.371	.317	.152	.373	.247	.520	.573

of that region remain at the bottom of national rankings of government spending for most functions, but they have shown great progress. State and local spending per capita in the Southeast was only 33 percent of the national average in 1902, but it was 80 percent of the national average in 1962.

Although some irony may appear in the simultaneous development of both greater national and regional uniformities in government spending, they may be viewed as common products of one basic experience. This is a growth in communications among policy makers of different states and several federal agencies, spurred on by nation-wide developments in the economy and in the attractions of federal grants-in-aid. State officials are emulating their counterparts in other states more now than in the past, and their emulation has both regional and national results. Improved interstate communications and improved professional training for administrators produce greater attention to both regional and national "models" of public policy. Associations of government officials have national and regional meetings that provide important interstate communications. There were only two of these organizations before 1900, and at least 46 by 1966.

Federal aids have increased many times in magnitude during this century, and they have provided models of public policy that have destroyed the isolation of individual government units. Yet federal aids have not destroyed regionalism. The regional offices of federal agencies carry on the bulk of communications with state and local officials, and they facilitate the development of regional variants in federally-aided projects. Other aspects of the federal-state relationship indicate that state and local governments *do not* behave like supplicants who obey the Washington paymaster. Instead, state and local officials maintain strong alliances with leaders in Congress and the federal administration. These alliances often reveal themselves in discretionary provisions which allow state and local policy-makers to design their own variations of federally-aided programs. Information about public assistance programs, in particular, reveal the presence of regional variations in federally-aided programs. Table V-1 shows that states in the Southeast score markedly below the national average in payments to the families of dependent children—even after controlling for the low level of economic development in that region. This program suffers from the taints of race and illegitimacy, and southern politicians reflect the prevailing norms in their region by applying stringent controls against AFDC payments.

SUMMARY AND CONCLUSIONS

When they look outside of their own governments for new ideas, public officials often follow the routine of regional consultation. Although the data is fragmentary, it suggests that state officials consult with their counterparts in neighboring states, and local officials look to neighboring communities within their own state when they seek expert advice. In the case of both state and local governments, however, those agencies which are innovative may consult with others in their "elite" group, no matter where their location.

The factors that support regional consultations include similarities in social problems, economic resources, and political climate; the expectation that comparisons within the neighborhood will prove to be locally relevant, easy to attain, and legitimate in the eyes of political elites; and the personal knowledge which neighboring officials have of one another.

By examining findings for several regions on 40 measures of policy, we identified certain shared traits that are not simply the product of shared economic characteristics. These shared policy traits may reflect officials' routine of seeking models for emulation from within their own region. Many regional patterns seem to have grown from historical experiences that were shared by neighboring states. The variety of these historical events suggest the various factors that have made regional routines accepted practice. Regional policy-norms trace their origins to such factors as the religious inclinations of first settlers, cultural traits of the population, geographical traits, racial conflict, and common experiences in politics and economics.

A test with state and local government spending levels since 1902 reveals that levels of government spending are becoming more uniform across the nation. However, regional partners are also becoming more alike in spending patterns. This dual finding suggests the growing importance of interstate communications and emulation, but it also suggests that regional patterns of consultation are guiding these processes.

NOTES

1. This chapter relies on my *Regionalism in American Politics* (Indianapolis: Bobbs-Merrill, 1969).

2. *Wisconsin's State and Local Tax Burden* (University of Wisconsin Tax Study Committee: Madison, 1959).

3. Jack L. Walker, "The Adoption of Innovations By the American States" Prepared for Presentation at the Conference on the Measurement of Public Policies in the American States, University of Michigan, July, 1968, mimeo.

4. The agencies surveyed were those with a budget of at least $1 million in 1966.

5. The districts chosen for interviewing were the 10 districts spending the most per pupil above the level estimated on the basis of several characteristics, and the 10 spending the least per pupil below the level estimated. The method of estimation was the selection of the greatest positive and negative residuals from a multiple regression analysis that employed the following independent variables: per capita personal income of district residents; percentage of adults in district with at least a high school education; percentage of adults voting in the most recent presidential election; and percentage of educational funds raised from local sources. We return to this survey in Chapter VII, where we use certain findings in discussing the superintendents' use of the spending-service cliche.

6. Walker, *op. cit.*

7. Nicholas A. Masters, Robert Salisbury, and Thomas H. Eliot, *State Politics and the Public Schools* (New York: Alfred A. Knopf, 1964), p. 21; cited in Walker, *op. cit.*

8. Thomas R. Dye, *Politics, Economics and the Public: Policy Outcomes in the American States* (Chicago: Rand McNally, 1966).

9. We first estimate each region's score on a policy variable by the regression formula:

$$Y = a + b_1X_1 + b_2X_2 + b_3X_3$$

In this formula, Y equals the estimated regional average on a measure of policy; X_1, X_2, and X_3 are the regional scores for each economic variable (per capita personal income, percent urban, and total personal income); and the a and b's are constants determined by a 48-state regression of the dependent variable with the three economic variables. The use of this formula with regional scores on the independent variables will produce an estimate (Y) of the policy score for each region. Then we compare this regional estimate with the actual regional average for the policy variable according to the simple formula:

$$\frac{\text{actual regional mean of Y}}{\text{regional mean estimated for Y}}$$

The more this ratio differs from 1.00, the region's score will be greater (or less) than is generally associated with its level of economic development. See *Regionalism in American Politics, op.cit.*, especially Chapters II, V, VI for a more complete description of the measurements, research techniques, and findings.

10. We shall make no effort to discuss each of the regional findings that are apparent in the data of Table VI-1. Those which are discussed portray several examples of the many historical, cultural, political and geographic factors that may support regional policy norms. The member states of each region are New England: Maine, New Hampshire, Vermont, Massachusetts, Rhode Island, Connecticut; Mid-Atlantic: New York, New Jersey, Pennsyl-

vania, Delaware, Maryland; Southeast: Virginia, West Virginia, North Carolina, South Carolina, Georgia, Florida, Kentucky, Tennessee, Alabama, Mississippi, Arkansas, Louisiana; Great Lakes: Ohio, Indiana, Michigan, Illinois, Wisconsin; Plains: Minnesota, Iowa, Missouri, North Dakota, South Dakota, Nebraska, Kansas; Southwest: Arizona, New Mexico, Oklahoma, Texas; Mountains: Montana, Idaho, Wyoming, Colorado, Utah; Far West: Washington, Oregon, Nevada, California.

11. Dye, *op. cit.,* p. 161.

12. It is not state or local governments, per se, that issue these bonds, but special corporations. They are "non-guaranteed" in the sense that the government does not guarantee their payment with its full faith and credit. Instead, the corporation established by the state to construct college dormitories, toll roads, or some other revenue-producing facility pledges the income from its about-to-be constructed project for the bonds' payment. Non-guaranteed bonds typically require the payment of a higher rate of interest than bonds guaranteed directly by government agencies, and this higher rate of interest works to keep borrowing low.

13. See, for example, V. O. Key, *Southern Politics in State and Nation* (New York: Alfred A. Knopf, 1949), p. 671 ff; Morton Grodzins, *The American Federal System,* Daniel J. Elazer, ed. (Chicago: Rand McNally, 1966), p. 379 ff; and Frank Munger, *American State Politics: Readings for Comparative Analysis* (New York: Crowell, 1966), pp. vii–viii.

VII.   The Spending-Service Cliche[1]

THE SPENDING-SERVICE CLICHE IS A ROUTINE WHICH EQUATES levels of expenditure with levels of service-output. In this chapter we explain some of the decision-makers' problems that encourage them to use the routine. Then we examine the assumed spending-service relationship that is at the heart of the routine. We assess the assumption for its validity, and identify some problems which the routine may impose upon policy-makers who use it.

The absence of an explicit test of previously described routines does not signify that we found them to be satisfactory. None of the routines considered in earlier chapters includes a clear set of assumptions or predictions that is so readily subject to analysis. They merely promise to simplify complex decisions, and offer nothing more explicit than an "acceptable" or "legitimate" decision. The routines that produce stable patterns of attitudes and voting behavior includes no prediction about policy-results that can be subject to a reliable test. Incremental budgeting likewise promises nothing more than a method to simplify decisions; in this case the decisions which allocate a government's revenues among competing agencies. There is no clear promise of political or policy results to follow the routine. The legislature's reliance on the governor's budget recommendations is similar in its lack of a standard against which to evaluate the practicioners' assumptions. The routine labeled "copy your neighbor" offers a way of choosing models that are relevant to one's own situation, but it does not promise to reward the user with any clear set of results.

The spending-service routine does promise a tangible reward for its users. It assumes a relationship between spending levels and service levels, and promises service improvements to officials who increase spending. We evaluate this promise by comparing levels of government spending with levels of public service. The assumed linkage is frequently absent. On the strength of this finding and some additional analysis, we conclude that policy-makers who use the spending-service routine may mislead them-

106

selves, hinder a more thorough analysis of the factors that affect service levels, and thereby retard program development.

FACTORS THAT LEAD DECISION-MAKERS TO RELY UPON THE SPENDING-SERVICE CLICHE

The spending-service cliche gets its support from the need of decision-makers for a device that will simplify reality. In this general attribute, the cliche resembles other routines that we have considered. Specific to the field program development, there are five principal elements which complicate decision-making:

1. the large number and complex interrelationships among the factors which actually have an influence on the character of services that an agency provides
2. the lack of information among decision-makers about these service factors.
3. the belief that some factors which influence the level of outputs are not conveniently subject to manipulation by public officials
4. the commonality of money as an element that may influence many potential service factors
5. a widespread belief among analysts and observers outside the decision-making arena that money is crucial among the factors that influence the level of service outputs.

1. Service determinants

Among the factors that can influence the nature of public services are the staff and leadership of an agency, its physical facilities, the clientele who are to be served, the organizational structure of the service agencies, the economy of the jurisdiction providing the service, and the political environment in which policy decisions are made. Although each of these factors may respond to the expenditures that are made for public services, they may also vary independently of expenditures. That is, they may respond to other influences besides the level of spending, and exert their own separate influence on the public service that is provided.

Several aspects of an agency's staff may influence the quality of service; the nature of training received by personnel, their sensitivity to clients' needs, and their motivation for professional advancement may add to or diminish the level of output associated with a certain expenditure. The simple factor of staff size, and the distribution of staff among the principal and auxiliary tasks performed in the agency can also affect the potential for rendering service. A high level of expenditure may permit the agency head to search for the "right combination" of training and motivation for each of the principal jobs within his organization, but money alone does not guarantee success. Indeed, the leader's own sensitivity to staff needs and his skill in using financial resources may be the key determinant that may (or may not) translate a good budget into a good staff.

The elements of physical plant and equipment that can affect an agency's service output include their compatibility with contemporary methods of providing service, their flexibility with respect to the multiple needs and changing demands of clients, and their durability in the face of heavy use. The nature of surroundings and the availability of modern equipment might contribute to the capacity of the staff to perform in a superior fashion. The durability of facilities affects the amount of money that must be spent on maintenance. If the plant and equipment cannot stand up to the clients, then the cost of repairs will reduce the expenditures that can be made on additional facilities or on staff improvement.

The distribution of service facilities with respect to their clients may also influence the quality of service that they provide. It may be trite to argue that public officials should locate institutions near the people they are designed to serve. However, in a number of states the personal interests of important legislators seem to be more important than the needs of clients in the location of hospitals, universities, parks, and new highways. Inconvenient locations increase the costs of transportation for clients and staff, and cut down the number of clients who actually use the facilities. Obtuse locations may force institutions to pay higher than average salaries in order to attract competent professionals to the staff. Some locations may discourage skilled professionals no matter what salary is offered.

The clients themselves may influence the service-outputs of an agency. Their number, the severity of their needs, their motivation, and their cultural and intellectual preparation can render the service expensive or efficient. Where the clients of an educational system come from culturally deprived families, for example, teachers will have further to go with a less receptive audience than is the case in school districts where the families are predominantly middle class, upwardly mobile, and appreciative of the opportunities offered by education. Also, some clients have sufficient wealth and motivation to supplement the expenditures on their services that are made by government agencies. Where parents' organizations make significant contributions for school libraries or recreational facilities, the public schools may allocate an unusually high proportion of its budget to useful auxiliary programs.

The economic features of available resources and market costs can influence the facilities or personnel that a jurisdiction can purchase. Variations in market costs can render skills or commodities more or less expensive, and thereby alter the items that can be purchased with a given budget. Changes in economic conditions can affect the level of funds that can be raised without resorting to oppressive levels of taxation, and influence the characteristics of clients who apply for services.

In the field of national defense, variations in cost can result from the nature of prospective antagonists. When the nature of likely opponents is large in number and presents varied conditions of military resources, terrain, and climate, then the cost of preparing one's own military capacity will be increased by the diverse nature of the contingencies that must be accommodated.

The organizational structure of service agencies may facilitate—or block—their response to the special needs of clients. A decentralized administration may permit a staff to adjust its performance to the opportunities provided by the available facilities. Yet decentralization may require a higher quality of local leadership than is actually available. And decentralization may entail some costly duplication of services. Where the budget is tight and the institutional officials are shallow in their resourcefulness, the centralized administration of services may produce the highest ratio of service outputs to government expenditures. The form of organization may also affect the economies of scale that a service unit might enjoy. Large institutions may lower the per-unit costs of service outputs. Large size may also add to the variety of professional specialists that an institution may employ, and thereby enrich the clients' experience. Yet size destroys intimacy, and there is some point at which institutions become too large; they encounter problems of coordination and the need to provide multiple units of the same type. There may be *diseconomies* of scale. Thus, flexibility in leadership and organization may be more important than size, per se, in the factors that influence service-outputs.

The political environment may have a profound influence on several factors that affect services. If it is customary to fill positions and make promotions on the basis of partisan support, then the staff may have few of the traits that are professionally desirable. Likewise in the location of new institutions. Where they are placed to satisfy the desire of powerful legislators, the institutions may be less adequate in providing services than if they were located with primary consideration to the needs of the clients. The values, attitudes, and perceptions of elected officials may serve as important intermediaries to the impact that clients' own needs and resources have on public services. Some politicians are particularly responsive to the needs for certain types of public service. They support certain professionals, promote the organizational changes that appear to be helpful, and protect the agency from the demands of special interest groups. The problem of such officials is to decide *which* professionals, *which* organizational changes, and *which* interest groups should receive support. These choices may depend on more information about the current situation than most politicians are likely to possess.

2. *Ignorance about service determinants*

The speculative nature of this discussion reveals the lack of hard information about those elements which affect public services. There is much folklore about the elements that will help to improve services, but there is little information about the results to be expected from certain combinations of ingredients under certain conditions. In a number of federal, state, and local agencies that have access to sophisticated staff assistance and electronic data processing equipment, efforts are being made to identify salient features which have a bearing on the level of services produced.[2] This work in itself suggests that numerous officials are concerned about unnecessary expenditures that are made because of an assumed equation between spending and services. In most cases, however, the identification of actual determinants of service levels is still in the exploratory stage. It is not sufficiently widespread among government agencies, and its techniques are not sufficiently well-accepted for it to have wide application. As we shall see below when we describe the results of interviews with policy-makers in the field of elementary and secondary education, there is a marked lack of agreement among officials in similar types of agencies—and with similar levels of professional training—about the elements that influence service levels. Instead of agreeing about what factors need to be developed or strengthened in order to produce a satisfactory level of output, officials seem to be groping among the possible influences and producing widely-divergent lists about the items to be given their attention.

3. Unmanipulable service determinants

Among the elements that seem likely to influence service levels, a number of them appear unamenable to direct manipulation by government officials. Because of this, decision-makers may be dissuaded from a thorough analysis of service determinants, and led to rely on the simple routine which assumes a spending-service relationship. We suggest above that the preparation of clients, their motivation for making the efforts that are part of the services to be rendered, the level of economic development in a community, and the attractiveness of a community as a residence for professional and technical personnel have a bearing on the services which an agency can render. Although each of these elements may be altered by long-range campaigns directed specifically at them, it is unlikely that these changes can be made the responsibility of service agencies who have other, more immediate goals. Moreover, the quality of past concern for each service helps to determine current outputs. Where a lack of attention in the past has left a small capital base on which current expenditures can grow, an agency is not likely to produce high quality services with its first large budget increase. Large expenditures for highways are not likely to produce a first-class road network where none has existed before. Where previous inattention to public higher education has left a state with a weak university, poorly equipped and run by tired but entrenched administrators, an across-the-board pay increase for the faculty will not produce any rapid improvement in its output.

4. The appeal of money as a common denominator among service determinants

In the face of the complexities which face the decision-maker who would undertake a thorough analysis of the elements that influence his agency's level of services, the routine of the spending-service cliche offers both simplicity and credibility. Although money, per se, does not affect levels of service, it seems reasonable to believe that money will purchase many of the commodities that do affect services. Money is not only a common denominator, but it is subject to manipulation by government officials. If the present level of service is not satisfactory, it is always possible—assuming sufficient resources or sufficient willingness to increase taxes—to spend more money. With additional dollars, officials can seek to recruit and/or train leaders and scientific-technical-professional personnel for their agencies; they can pay existing personnel enough money to make it difficult for them to accept employment elsewhere; they may offer financial inducements so that personnel will accept changes in organizational structure or changes in agency norms; and they can buy the material and talents necessary to construct and maintain attractive and functional physical facilities. Unfortunately, the temptation and the willingness to spend more money may not solve the service problem. Not only are some service determinants not subject to alteration by current spending, but it is also unclear which of the purchasable commodities—and how much of each—will do the job that is desired.

5. Popular acceptance of the spending-service relationship

One of the factors that helps to make the spending-service cliche attractive to decision-makers is its popularity among those who observe and analyze public policy. Journalists frequently rank government activities on some readily-available financial scale. Total spending, expenditures per client, or per capita are favorite subjects of comparison. Several academic social scientists with solid reputations as scholars, consultants, and government executives also give high marks to the spending-service cliche. In much of the literature that examines government expenditures in the United States, we can find the assumption that spending provides the primary stimulant for public services. In *1400 Governments,* Robert C. Wood defends his examination of revenues and expenditures because they "reflect the scope and character of (local) government operations."[3] In *Public School Finance,* Jesse Burkhead claims that "for the most part, expenditure variations reflect genuine differences in the calibre of educational services provided."[4] And Philip H. Burch writes that money is "the alpha and the omega" in the highway field.[5] A number of other scholars who claim to examine the "outputs" of American governments imply that expenditures coincide with service levels by their willy-nilly mixture of spending and service analyses.[6] Most writers who assume the expenditure-service correspondence fail to test their belief. On some occasions they overlook contrary data from their own tables. In his study of school finance, for example, Jesse Burkhead is not troubled by the lack of significant statistical relationships between four measures of educational expenditure and such likely indicators of service as the salary of beginning teachers, the insurable value of school property, and the number of full time employees in auxiliary services.[7]

THE ROUTINE AS EXPRESSED BY POLICY-MAKERS

There is little direct evidence about the acceptance of the spending-service cliche among policy-makers. Perhaps because the cliche has such wide acceptance among scholars who are interested in public finance, it has not received a thorough examination. The most powerful evidence for officials' use of the spending-service cliche is the apparent absence of widely-held notions about non-monetary determinants of public service outputs. Scholars and policy-makers express the counter-cliche that "money is not everything," but they have not proceeded far with the identification of non-monetary service determinants. The analyses that have been attempted thus far indicate that service determinants are highly particularistic. That is, the factors that influence the nature of services produced are important in a limited context of certain services, agency personnel, and clients.[8] Thus, policy makers and scholars have no list of service determinants that has the simplicity or the appeal of the spending-service cliche. In the absence of any better information, policy-makers can only seek additional funds when they wish to make major improvements in their service-outputs, and rely on their own (usually untested) assessments in allocating the new funds among various items of personnel, equipment, and facilities.

There is some evidence about the use of the spending-service cliche among a sample of school superintendents in the state of Georgia. As part of a larger study of spending and other service determinants of educational services in that state, an interview schedule was designed to elicit the opinions of these superintendents about the components of "good" or "high quality" educational programs, and the factors that produce these programs. Twenty school superintendents were selected in a way to represent both high- and low-spending districts.[9] The size and the nature of the survey means that it is only an exploratory investigation of the spending-service cliche as it is viewed by policymakers. However, the findings are sufficiently consistent with other information to suggest that the cliche is widely held among officials.

Two questions asked about the factors that provide the makings of high quality programs. The first asked: *What factors help to produce "good" or "high quality" programs?* The second inquiry followed a series of questions that asked superintendents to estimate the size of an optimum budget (i.e., a budget that would provide for needs above those permitted by present expenditures): *What, specifically, would you spend the additional money for, i.e., the money that is not included in your present budget, but which would be in your optimum budget?* After each of these questions, the respondents were asked to rank-order the items mentioned. Table VII-1 summarizes the responses to the two questions.

The principal findings of this survey show: (1) Georgia school superintendents are most likely to list money among the factors that produce high quality educational programs; and (2) their other nominations show little agreement about the nonmonetary ingredients of successful programs. Fourteen of the superintendents named money as one of the prime ingredients of quality programs, and they ranked it high among their nominations. Their statements varied from one respondent to the next, but their

TABLE VII-1

Responses of Georgia School Superintendents to Questions About the Ingredients of Quality Education

	What factors help produce good or high quality programs?		What, specifically, would you spend the additional money for, i.e., the money that is not included in your present budget, but which would be in your optimum budget?	
	number of nominations	average rank	number of nominations	average rank
qualified teachers	12	1.3	5	1.4
adequate financing	14	2.2	0	
leadership	4	1.8	0	
supportive environment	9	2.6	9	2.2
curriculum improvement	6	2.7	9	1.7
teacher–pupil ratio	3	1.7	11	3.0
equipment, facilities	4	2.5	5	3.4
inservice training	1	3.0	7	2.7
auxiliary personnel	1	3.0	8	3.1
teachers salary	0		3	5.7
other	1	6.0		

theme was consistent: Adequate financing is essential to a successful program.

More money and the prudent use thereof.

Adequate financing of program.

More state, federal and local money.

It all boils down to money; we can't compete with larger systems; we don't get enough money but the lay people think we are getting more.

Although Georgia school superintendents agree on the need for adequate funds, they do not agree on the items to purchase. Several recognize that money alone will not provide an adequate program. The first response above states that a "prudent" allocation is important. Some admitted that increased funds might not improve their programs. One respondent in a rural county that is suffering population decline commented: "If funds were made available I would attempt to hire better qualified teachers. (However) this would not likely induce many to work in this system."

Diversity is the distinguishing characteristic of the nominations for non-monetary ingredients of high quality programs. Most officials would seek more "qualified" teachers and administrators, but they make no clear indication about the "qualification" to pursue. Several superintendents named higher teacher salaries; a larger number of teachers; changes in the curriculum; more and better equipment and facilities; in-service training; auxiliary personnel in child psychology, remedial reading, art, and athletics. Several superintendents would improve their vocational training programs in order to satisfy the needs of students frustrated by academic programs. One superintendent would improve the athletic program in order to build spirit and dissuade potential dropouts. The variety of nominations reveal one of the primary bulwarks of the spending-service cliche. Officials do not agree on the substantive features that comprise a satisfactory program of education. Their professional training has not provided a clear set of guidelines about the factors which are likely to return a high service output in return for budget investments. However, money is a common factor in the complex environment of public education. It will purchase many elements that appear to be ingredients of high-quality education. The acceptance of this as a common factor may actually hinder the research necessary to identify the most important service determinants.

A study about educational spending and its correlates in 163 Georgia school districts provides further evidence of the diffuse conception about items to be purchased.[10] There are weak statistical relationships between spending per pupil and a number of variables that measure likely service determinants: the value of plant and equipment; teacher salaries; teacher-pupil ratio; the incidence of well-qualified teachers; and local effort in surpassing minimum state requirements. Policy-makers are choosing different combinations of elements to purchase with their expenditures. A certain level of expenditure does not mean that the superintendent has purchased a certain combination of items. Officials agree on the need for expenditures, but they seem to have no consistent notion about what they should buy.

It is not only in the school districts of one southern state where officials are without clear understanding of the factors that will produce the kinds of service outputs they desire. In education and other fields, the diffuse nature of service outputs and the large number and complex nature of potential service determinants, hinders the precise assessment of what an agency should produce, and how it should control its production. Many government agencies have difficulty in determining what it is they want to produce. Their difficulty stems not so much from fuzzy heads as it stems from the need to consider both *primary goals,* and the variety of implications (*subgoals*) that are associated with each major goal. The United States Departments of State and Defense have far greater resources that can be used for program analysis than do the school districts of Georgia. In Washington, the barrier to understanding service determinants is not a lack of analytic skills, but the complexity of the problem. The following excerpt was written by an expert on military policy, and was reprinted by a Committee of the United States Senate:

The utility of the (cost-effectiveness) technique depends very importantly on the completeness with which costs and benefits are analyzed. I stress particularly costs other than money, for these can be of great variety and, it seems to me, they are easily lost sight of. They may be political, as when a particular choice causes great inconvenience to an ally, or military, as when choice engenders a sharp decline in

the morale of service. Surely, service morale is an asset and its defla-
tion is, as such, a disadvantage. We might want to accept this disadvantage if the net benefits of a choice promise to be very substantial,
but we should hardly ignore or neglect it. To the extent that costs
and benefits cannot be measured with accuracy, and to the extent
that the problem is one of deciding, in an inherently subjective manner, between different sets of costs and benefits, *problems of choice are
insusceptible to rigorous economic analysis* [italics added]. A second
great limitation of the cost-effectiveness approach results from imperfect information. In the military area, various incalculable uncer-
tainties must be faced often. Costs may be uncertain, technology
uncertain, and the reactions and capabilities of potential enemy
nations are apt to be uncertain. This last uncertainty is of particular
import; it is imperative that military choices be examined within
a framework of interaction. An opponent's response to our choices
may, after all, curtail or altogether nullify the advantages we seek.
Nor is it enough to recognize the conflict aspects of the problem.
The possibilities of tacit or formal cooperation may be equally
significant.[11]

SOME TESTS OF THE SPENDING-SERVICE CLICHE

There are profound problems to be encountered in testing the
spending-service cliche. As observers of government agencies, we
have no clearer idea than their officials about the features that
comprise "good services." Like them, we lack a standard of
excellence against which we can compare actual outputs of service and the levels of spending associated with the outputs. Not
only are there disagreements about what kinds of service levels
agencies should strive to attain, but there are related disagreements about the proper units to be used in measuring what the
agencies actually produce.

The closest we come to a test of the spending-service linkage is
the examination of statistical associations between several measures of spending, and other measures that assess certain aspects
of the output expected from each type of service. In order to
accept the spending-service cliche as it is often stated ("The level
of spending in a jurisdiction determines the level of public services"), the government units showing high (or low) levels of
spending should show consistently high (or low) scores on most
measures of service output. Because it is necessary to compare the
expenditures and services of government units that produce similar kinds of outputs, we must limit this test to the spending and
services of state and local governments.

The "outputs" of public service are the final stages in the production of program activities. They pertain not to the level of expenditures, the character of personnel, or the value of facilities. "Outputs" are the products of all the interacting "inputs" that go into the service process. The outputs of different fields are necessarily defined in terms of the service that is produced. Some measure the amount of benefits or services provided per client. Some measure the units of service in relation to population. Some measure the incidence of beneficiaries among people likely to use a service. Others measure the rate at which a program is performed. Others assess services by the frequency with which the population chooses to use a program. And some assess services indirectly by measuring the continued existence of phenomena that activities are designed to control.

Two studies in different contexts have shown that the relationships between government expenditures and the outputs of public service are neither strong nor pervasive. The study of 163 Georgia school districts shows only weak relationships between expenditures per pupil and two measures of educational output: the percentage of enrollees who are attracted to attend daily; and the percentage of high school enrollees who are attracted to remain in school until graduation.[12] Another study of state and local governments' spending and service outputs from across the country found that only 16 of 27 output measures (59 percent) showed sizable relationships with government spending.[13]

Several spending-service relationships are negative. This means that high scores on spending correspond with low scores on the measure of service. In the highway field the mileage per capita of rural roads and traffic deaths per capita are negatively related with state and local government highway spending. Apparently it is the low spending states that develop the most extensive systems of rural roads. Low spending states also experience the most enviable record of highway safety. In the field of public safety, the crime rates for rape, robbery, burglary, larceny, and auto theft are low where spending is low, while high crime rates coexist with high spending. It is unlikely that high (or low) spending brings about high (or low) crime rates. The incidence of crime probably works upon the spending level. States with little crime feel comfortable with relatively low per capita expenditures for public safety.

The evidence is also discouraging for the expectation that an increase in spending will produce a clear improvement in services.[14] Only ten measures of 1957–62 change in services showed sizable positive relationships with 1957–62 changes in spending. Perhaps the lag between an increase in spending and a change in service levels is greater than five years. Or perhaps an increase in spending is not powerful enough to cope with all of the nonfinancial elements in bringing about a change in the nature of services.

Several nonfinancial characteristics show stronger, and more consistent relationships with services than do government spending.[15] In the field of education, output is highest where there is the greatest incidence of adults with at least a high school education. Perhaps the parents' concern for education makes itself felt on their children and on school personnel. Where parents have an education, children are well prepared for school, and administrators may have greater incentive to provide a high quality program. Highway mileage per capita varies directly with the incidence of motor vehicles, while road safety varies inversely with the incidence of vehicles. Perhaps high levels of traffic produce more accidents and, through intermediate influence on the political process, more road mileage.

The characteristics of personal income and urbanization show strong positive relationships with several measures of public service. The demands and resources associated with personal well-being and urbanization may incline state and local governments to high quality educational activities plus generous and broad coverage in public assistance programs. There are contrary findings in the highway and natural resource fields. High-income urban states score *low* on total road mileage and urban mileage, per capita, but they score high on the early completion of the Interstate System, and road safety. Urban states traditionally have been less inclined to focus on road building than the rural states, but the early start of urban states on the Interstate System may reflect a changing emphasis in their politics. With population congestion and auto travel reaching increasing heights, the urban states may be forced to take speedy advantage of new highway programs. High income urban states also tend to score below average on measures of fish and wildlife activities. Demands and opportunities for outdoor recreation are typically associated with rural residents and wide-open spaces.

SUMMARY AND CONCLUSIONS

The spending-service cliche simplifies the decisions of policy-makers who seek to maintain or improve their agency's level of services. It promises service improvement via increases in spending, but it leaves to the decision-maker the job of specifying which types of items—and how much of each—he will purchase. However, the spending-service cliche leaves the policy-maker without guidance after the point when he advocates spending increases. The routine simplifies some decisions in the presence of complex factors pertaining to the ingredients of an effective program, but it does not compensate entirely for the ignorance of the decision-maker.

The interviews with Georgia school superintendents show that they agree about the importance of money for school programs, but they do not agree about the items to be purchased. This same finding is reflected in weak statistical relationships between the level of spending and the incidence of factors that might improve services. School districts operating at the same level of expenditures use their resources in a variety of ways with respect to teacher salaries, in the teacher-pupil ratio, the selection of highly trained teachers, the decision to surpass state-established minimum standards, and the value of plant and facilities.

Comments made by an expert in defense policy suggest that it is not only a lack of sophistication that precludes our understanding service-determinants. Instead, the complexity of outputs that agencies produce—in education as well as defense—can hinder one's comprehension of which factors other than money actually work to produce an agency's goals. Compared to the difficulties in making an analysis of the factors which actually affect service outputs, the spending-service cliche prescribes simple decisions. Officials find much reinforcement from their colleagues and from outside observers when they claim that an increase in funds is necessary to improve services. However, they may undercut their own potential for analysis and program improvement by continuing to assume a simplistic spending-service relationship.

Several tests of the spending-service assumption prove disappointing. For the most part, there are only weak relationships between measures of spending (in Georgia school districts or in the aggregates of state and local governments across the country) and measures of service levels. In the case of several measures of service, the most critical determinants appear to be social and economic characteristics that are not directly amendable to manipulation by government officials.

Hopefully, findings like our's will alert decision-makers, outside observers of public services, and students of political science to the dangers in assuming a clear relationship between an agency's level of expenditure and its service outputs. Yet we have not meant to strike at expenditures as a device to improve service outputs. Our results *do not* mean that focused increases in spending will fail to improve particular services or particular institutions. Furthermore, the results do not strike at the variety of reasons for increasing spending that do not assume an early increase in services. These include the desire to keep salaries of public employees equivalent to those of people in comparable nongovernmental positions; and the desire to improve staff or physical plant for the sake of obtaining service improvements over the long range or for the sake of avoiding a deterioration of services.

Many of the factors that compete with expenditures for influence over services are *not* subject to manipulation in the short run. These include the number or character of clients and the social-economic nature of a community. Expenditures may have only a tangential influence on public services, but expenditures are subject to the actions of government officials. Increases in spending provide a useful mechanism for improving public service. However, officials should not expect rapid success in the face of difficult social or economic conditions, and unless they can make informed decisions in altering spending patterns, increases in spending may not have any impact on service levels.

NOTES

1. The discussion in this chapter relies on my *The Politics of Taxing and Spending* (Indianapolis: Bobbs-Merrill, 1969), Chapter VI.

2. See "Planning-Programming-Budgeting Symposium," *Public Administration Review*, XXVI (December 1966); David Novick, ed.,; *Program Budgeting: Program Analysis and the Federal Budget* (Washington: U.S. Government Printing Office, 1965); and Robert Dorfman, ed., *Measuring Benefits of Government Investment* (Washington: The Brookings Institution, 1965).

3. Robert C. Wood, *1400 Governments* (Garden City: Anchor Books, 1961), p. 35.

4. Jesse Burkhead, *Public School Finance* (Syracuse: Syracuse University Press, 1965), p. 50.

5. Philip C. Burch, *Highway Revenue and Expenditure Policy in the United States* (New Brunswick: Rutgers University Press, 1962), p. 34.

6. Thomas R. Dye, *Politics, Economics and the Public: Policy Outcomes in the American States* (Chicago: Rand McNally, 1966); Richard E. Dawson and James A. Robinson, "Interparty Competition, Economic Variables, and Welfare Policies in the American States," *Journal of Politics*, 25 (May 1963), pp. 265–89.

7. Burkhead, *op. cit.*, pp. 50–75.

8. See the literature cited in note #2 above.

9. For a more complete report about this study see my "Environment, Policy, Output and Impact: Problems of Theory and Method in the Analysis of Public Policy," a paper presented at the Annual Meeting of the American Political Science Association, 1968.

10. See the paper cited in note 9 above.

11. Klaus Knorr," On The Cost-Effectiveness Approach to Military Research and Development," *Bulletin of the Atomic Scientists*, XXII (November 1966), reprinted in "Planning-Programming-Budgeting: Selected Comment," a Committee Print of the Subcommittee on National Security and International Operations of the U.S. Senate Committee on Government Operations (Washington: U.S. Government Printing Office, 1967).

12. See the paper cited in note 9 above.

13. *The Politics of Taxing and Spending, op. cit.*, Chapter VI.

14. See my "Government Expenditures and Public Services in the American States," *American Political Science Review*, LXI (December 1967), pp. 1066–77.

15. See *The Politics of Taxing and Spending, op. cit.*, Chapter VI.

VIII. Political Parties: Amateurs Without Routines

> . . . it is difficult to escape the overriding weakness and problems of American party organization. It is even difficult to take it seriously in an analytical or scholarly enterprise.[1]

THIS DISCUSSION OF POLITICAL PARTIES AND THE LATER DISCUSsion of interest groups stand apart from the earlier chapters. Instead of focusing on the routines of voters or policy-makers, we make an analysis of features that hinder the development of routines.

Recall from the discussion in Chapter I that routines simplify complex situations for decision-makers are used by most individuals for whom they are relevant, and provide stability to political systems. Here we argue that certain features must be present in the decision-making apparatus in order for routines to develop. Some degree of stability, integration, or continuity in personnel seems necessary before routines will arise in a complex decision situation. As in previous chapters, our focus will be the American context. Our findings may not apply to other types of political parties that can be found in certain foreign settings. American political parties are neither stable, integrated, nor continuous. The totality of each major party (i.e., the numerous committees, groups, and individuals who align themselves with the parties' electoral tasks) shows frequent dissonance between national and state levels, and at each level there is conflict between transient groups that affiliate with the party in order to support particular candidates or causes. Although there are paid workers with long tenure in each party, they do not dominate policy-making. There is no systematic training for party personnel. Individuals serve informal apprenticeships, but they do not develop into a cadre of leaders sharing a specific body of knowledge or certain codes of behavior.

In the American parties, persons do create decision rules to help make complex decisions. However, the discontinuities in training, background, and purpose preclude the wide sharing of these rules. Different rules claim to prescribe for similar types of decision. Moreover, the decision rules do not show the isolation from environmental stimuli that we have found for routines. Recall that incremental budget-makers start calculating from their own prior decisions, nearly irrespective of what happens in politics or in the economy. In contrast, party officials often seem badgered by an excessive and continuous analysis of their environment, in ways that sometimes provoke contradictory—and perhaps disastrous—changes in campaign strategy. We shall label the decision rules of parties *principles* in order to distinguish them from routines. Principles are acquired by individuals during their learning process as party leaders, but they are not widely shared. Principles are not consistently helpful in decision-making. Principles are less precise than routines in the behavior they advise. Like simple homilies that are stitched into the samplers of young girls who intend to be virtuous, political principles are seldom helpful in concrete situations. Several principles appear to contradict one another, and they provide few cues as to which should be used under each set of conditions. Principles may guide the decisions of some individuals, but their status is not firm and they are more readily subject to change or abandonment than routines.

Political parties in the United States are diffuse entities that include party officials, candidates for public office, incumbent office holders who associate themselves with the party label, individual citizens who count themselves as party adherents and donate their time and money to the party or its candidates for office, and countless other citizens who identify themselves in varying degrees of intensity as members or supporters of the party's candidates. In Chapter II, we described some routines which individual party supporters use in the maintenance of their party identification and the use of their party identification in the selection of candidates and policy opinions that will receive their support. In this chapter, the focus of attention is the *party as organization*. This is an abstraction that includes many varieties of individuals and decision-making units that concern themselves with making party policy or conducting election campaigns. Party organizations have shown stability over time. As we noted in Chapter II, the Democratic and Republican parties antedate almost all of the governmental regimes that currently control the most powerful nations of the world. Some party organizations do exhibit integrated, continuous elites that make some decisions with the help of rules that are shared within the party organization. However, most party organizations in individual states and communities appear to be weakly-jointed organs governed by small cadres of activists rather than by tightly-knit hierarchies. The stability of party form and structure does not denote the stability of decision rules. It is the thesis of this chapter that party organizations generally lack articulate, widely-shared decision-rules that can be labeled as "routines."

FACTORS INHIBITING THE DEVELOPMENT OF PARTY ROUTINES

American party organizations exist at the confluence of several forces that hinder the development of routine decision-rules. Some of these forces originate in the electorate and take the form of complex loyalties and cross pressures among the voters. These make it difficult for party leaders to assess the impact of campaign devices on the voters' predispositions. Other forces come from within the parties themselves. The dependence of national parties on cooperation from the state and local levels, the prevailing lack of party discipline, and the lack of a strong professional staff having control over party finance or staffing each get in the way of concerted action. The tools that politicians use during campaigns can further discourage the development of routine decision-rules. Newspapers, radio, and television are not predictable in their impact on voters, and public-opinion polling requires sophisticated skills for both the survey and the interpretation of results. Where the necessary talents are not available to a candidate's team, the poorly contrived use of advertising or polling may hinder the development of firm notions about the tactics that are most useful in different campaign settings. Finally, the candidates vary widely in their own political training and in their personal skills. To the extent that campaign strategies must be put into operation by unmalleable candidates, the strategies cannot be well-ordered routines. They must be tailored to the personnel and issues of the situation.

The problems involved in campaigning suggest that the talents required are those of the artist instead of the scientist. This is significant, because the artist creates distinctive objects with the materials at hand. He does not use routines. If he did, he would be a manufacturer. Despite the pollsters, the advertising agencies, and the public-relations men who use the methods of social science to analyze the voting public and adjust campaign tactics, party politics in the United States has a large ingredient of art.[2]

In studying the phenomena of campaign, election, and results, the political scientist does well to consider the displays of intuition that distinguish the artistry of the truly expert politician from the unimaginative techniques of the political hack. No doubt the pollsters can inform the candidate within reasonably certain limits where he is strong or weak (if he has adequate funds to sponsor a reliable poll), and the advertising men can suggest the "image" which they believe appeals to voters. Nixon's eyebrows can be trimmed to make him look less like the villain of an early western, and Kennedy's hair can be cut to give him a less boyish appearance. In every election, however, there are a number of factors that cannot be accurately reduced to figures, much less manipulated, by the new men of commercial political "science." These "unknowns" remain the province of the professional politician—the "inside dopester," if you will—whose "art" is manifest in his ability to feel or intuit the unknown factors through extrasensory political antennae.

In this section we shall examine several of the features that hinder the development of routines in political parties. In the order of our discussion, the barriers to routines are found in the nature of the electorate, in the party organization, in the media employed by campaign leaders, and in the character of party candidates.

1. The electorate

In the diffuse American electorate, party leaders encounter a number of problems that make it difficult for them to predict the results of their campaign strategy. As a result, there is little basis of *experience with analysis* that can help in the development of routines. The numerous loyalties of the voters are the prime source of confusion. Not only are there many diverse groups having politically relevant attachments to ethnic groups, social classes, occupational groups, regional norms, and numerous features of political ideology, but many combinations of these attachments can be found in individual voters. The result is that politicians must predict the likely behavior of "groups" conceived as pure social types (e.g., Negroes, Jews, bankers, union members), and "groups" conceived as individuals who are attached to several designations at the same time. When the impetus associated with each of one man's several loyalties would lead him in the same political direction, the prediction will be simple. Most of the time, it is not necessary to make separate calculations for the voters who combine the traits of Catholic, working class, urban, and union-member, because these traits lead in the same (Democratic) direction. The task of the politician is more difficult when large numbers of people are placed in a conflict situation. An example occurred in the 1960 Presidential election, when middle- and upper-class Catholics found themselves forced to choose between the Democratic inclination associated with their religious identification, and the Republican loyalties triggered by their occupational and social class affiliations.

Among the loyalties of American voters are their feelings of attachment toward a political party. Indeed, we saw in Chapter II that routine partisanship is a predictable component of elections. Yet the campaigner must convince his party members to vote in this particular election, and to honor their traditional party allegiance. Party allegiance interacts with numerous other loyalties in determining if a voter with cast his ballot, and which candidate he will support. "Party discipline" is not rigid among the voters of America, just as we shall see below it is not rigid among the officials and candidates of the major parties. Moreover, there remains a significant minority of voters who hold no firm party tie (see pp. 34–39). This *swing vote* may hold the key to a candidate's election. The majority's allegiance to the Democratic party does not guarantee success to the nominees of that party. And, of course, the routine of party allegiance does not provide much guidance to campaigners during their quest for the party nomination.

The lack of ideological attachments among most voters complicates the task of predicting their behavior and developing campaign routines. Survey research has found only a small minority of voters who respond as "ideologues," even when the test of ideological attachment is not demanding.[3] Voters generally make up their mind by something other than what the politicians say about issues. Many voters decide more by the way in which a policy-stance is explained, or by the personality and style of the candidate, or by the popular "feeling" that is aroused by current economic or international events. These elements of style or circumstance are far more difficult than issues to lay before the voters. The very number of items to which voters may respond makes the tasks of the campaigner difficult to routinize. Tactics of style, in particular, do not readily lend themselves either to analysis or routine application.

One of the creatures that makes life difficult for the politician is the "alienated voter." Where he occurs in large numbers his presence may set the tone for campaigning and makes campaigning even more unpredictable than usual. The traits of the alienated voter include distrust of public officials and politicians, and a profound sense of his own inability to have an impact on public life. He views candidates as being corrupt or incompetent, and the community as being controlled by a power elite of corrupt politicians, self-serving businessmen, and racketeers. He believes that candidates become obligated to those who make financial contributions, and that it makes little difference which candidate wins office. In his eyes the electoral process is a mockery of democracy since the voter has no real control over the affairs of government.[4] The alienated voter sees the "ideal candidate" as one who is "honest, sincere, nonpolitical, not heavily financed, 'inexperienced,' 'nonprofessional' and not too well known."[5] Where the alienated voter is prominent in the population, politicians are aware of his presence and campaign accordingly. The alienated voter distrusts overt partisanship and he may lead party officials and candidates to mask whatever semblance of common viewpoint may unite those who identify with their party. Style becomes all-important in the campaign. Because voters distrust the "promises" of politicians, issues are de-emphasized. The *style campaign* even more than the issue campaign is the province of the artist, and hinders the development of routines that might guide tactical decisions.

The response of the electorate to the "style" of a candidate is not easy to predict. Although one can estimate the proportion of voters who might be swayed by an appeal to abolish rent control, a programmatic issue, we can suggest no method of determining whether a reserved demeanor on television will be interpreted as "statesmanlike" or vacuous.[6]

2. The party organization

Among the several aspects of party organization that hinder the development of routines, the most prominent is a lack of discipline. This shows itself in many ways. We have already discussed the lack of discipline among the electorate. Although most voters regularly support "their" party, this is more a reflection of political habit and convenience than a response to a code of party membership. The most apparent characteristic of American parties is that they have no members, per se. They receive the votes of "supporters" who feel a party tie. Only a few state or local parties have made an effort to sign up members, collect dues, or distribute identity cards. Party leadership is provided by individuals and groups who may be motivated more by their loyalty to individual candidates or causes than by their loyalty to the party itself. The result is a crazy-quilt of segmental loyalties that sometime conflict with one another.

Like many other large and complex organizations, political parties contain many individuals and groups with their own goals. Voters, candidates, precinct workers, advertising specialities, pollsters, and state and national committee members have varying perspectives about the importance of winning an election, maintaining cordial relationships, analyzing a public opinion survey, writing a speech, or setting up an advertising program. The election of the party nominee is not uniformly held as the primary goal. Individuals adhere to parties for diverse personal and professional reasons, and may assign primary value to some aspect of a campaign.[7] While the leaders of other complex organizations may ameliorate the problems of diverse members' goals by enforcing discipline, the American parties lack central units that are powerful enough to control recruiting, select sub-group leaders, and operate the party budget.

State laws that govern party organizations help to perpetuate a lack of discipline within the parties. Such laws typically give no controls over the selection of members to party officials. Instead, they give the election of local committeemen and other party officers, as well as the selection of party nominees to the voters who take part in primary elections. Increasingly, state laws have sought to "democratize" political parties, and in doing so they have inhibited the development of professional organizations that are capable of developing routine decision-rules. Although some state or local parties may used regularized procedures for selecting leaders or making nominations for public office, laws requiring open party meetings and primaries make these procedures uncertain. Also, the constant turnover in the activists who lead some party groups makes it unlikely that routine procedures can become firmly embedded, and passed on to successive generations or party leaders.

Related to the parties' lack of discipline is their decentralized structure. The national parties are composed of 50 state parties, which are themselves composed of parties based in countries, municipalities, or legislative districts. Nominations and financial support for state and local offices come from state or local party organizations, which may be nothing more than a personal organization focused on the career of one politician. The nomination and much of the money for presidential campaigns also depends on decisions that are made in state and local parties. There is no cadre of national party officials that issue policy directives to states or localities. Potential nominees for national office must pay homage to the state or local party officials who control the votes at the national party convention. National party leaders lack any financial sanction over state organizations. There is more money transferred from state and local groups to the National Party Committees than is transferred downward from the center.[8]

The national party offers few tangible incentives for state or local cooperation, and holds no formal sanction over state or local recalcitrants. Some congressmen and governors have campaigned openly in opposition to the presidential nominee of their party. At one time this problem was peculiarly Democratic, with liberal presidential nominees expecting to write-off the support of conservative Southerners. But the 1964 contest showed that Republicans also have a major problem with party discipline. Governors

Rockefeller and Romney, Senator Javits, and New York's Mayor Lindsay were noticeably absent from those who supported Barry Goldwater.

The ideological diversity within each party has been accepted as a virtue, and perpetuated by party leaders who make their platforms ambiguous in order to cast a broad appeal. American voters are viewed as being nonideological with attitudes on most issues that type them as "middle of the road." Most voters are within striking distance of appeals from either party. The result has been diffuse and ambiguous pronouncements, which have lessened whatever chance the parties have to make their members, officers and candidates more disciplined in their support of common principles.[9] Partly because of their ideological diversity, American parties are characterized by pragmatic office-seekers who put a premium on flexibility and the capacity to make the campaign adjustments that are necessary for electoral success. It is unlikely that parties will develop strong, permanent staffs that would desire—or be able—to maintain a coherent set of philosophical principles.[10]

Instead of large staffs with experts skilled in polling voters and advising candidates, American politicians often prefer the independence of their own organizations. A product of this independence is amateurism. One amateur campaigner bragged of his native ability to intuit the voters' wishes.[11]

I've traveled the circuit five times since January. I've talked to all types of people: taxi-cab drivers and workers, workers' meetings and people that are just—you know, that you happen to run into, strike up a conversation.

On the basis of this sampling procedure, the candidate (for a statewide office in Massachusetts) concluded that he could expect 120–125,000 votes, and would win in the cities of Worcester, New Bedford, Fall River, Salem, Somerville, Cambridge, and Malden. He actually received 76,539 votes, and the only city he carried was Malden, his home town.

Another product of amateurism is the contradictory shifting in tactics during a campaign. This may occur as competitive groups of advisors alternate as being the candidate's favorites.[12] It is this lack of a professional staff, perhaps more than any factor, which hinders the development of routines in American political parties.

With the responsibility for data gathering, evaluation and the choice of strategies left in the hands of transient supporters, it is hardly likely that routine decision processes will develop and find wide acceptance.

A prominent exception to the general absence of discipline in party organizations occurs in political machines. Some of these machines have been identified with lasting organizations (Tammany Hall), some have been governed by well-known personalities who seem to thrive in the public eye and enjoy the reputation of "genial rascality,"[13] and some have been led by dominant persons who marshal their resources as unspectacular but thorough technicians (Chicago's Richard Daley). At the core of the disciplined machine are ward and precinct workers who maintain close contact with the voters of their district. For these voters, the machine offers jobs, a favorable introduction to a social welfare agency, contracts with the local government, or an emergency donation for food or rent. The well-run machine also has rewards to satisfy its foot soldiers and sergeants who deliver the vote of masses, and other devices to select and promote its candidates for public office.

Although party machines are prominent exceptions to the general rule that party organizations are unstructured, they are few and declining in number. A prominent student of political parties writes that "machines have always been something of a genetic 'sport' among American political parties."[14] And with several changes in political affairs during the last 40 years, machines appear to be becoming even less typical among party organizations. The events that account for the decline of the machine include the development of the "welfare state" and the loss of incentives for political organizations to provide welfare benefits; the adoption of civil service reforms which limit the amount of personnel patronage available to party leaders; and the increasing skill requirements for government positions that weaken partisanship as a desirable criteria for appointment.

Even if regular decision procedures become well established in certain machines or other state or local party organizations, they are unlikely to spread to many separate organizations and thus acquire the characteristics of "routines." There are too many state and local parties which are undisciplined in their conception of, or attachment to, a clear set of party goals. There is a diffuseness in party organizations that is not apparent in budget agencies, legislatures, or some other policy-making organs of American governments. The individual voter generally seems to be a more well-integrated and consistent decision-making organism than most party organizations. The routines we have found in voters and policy-making units of government appear more wide-spread than any decision rules which have been observed in party organizations. "The modern party structure is indeed a hybrid, not conforming well to . . . expectations."[15]

3. Campaign media

Several characteristics of the media that parties use in their election campaigns hinder the development of routines. The media include public opinion polls (which feed information from the voters to the party); and newspapers, radio, and television (which transmit information from the parties to the voters). In part, the problems associated with these media result from the lack of professional talent in party organizations. However, the media present some problems which may limit the routinization of party activity, no matter what changes would—or could—be made in party structure and personnel.

Under optimum conditions, public opinion polling can provide five kinds of information:

1. The image of the candidate as he is perceived by the electorate
2. The identity of the areas (states, counties, or neighborhoods) where the candidate would be likely to improve his poll with increased activity
3. The nature of issues which have the greatest relevance for each category of citizens
4. An understanding of voter reaction to particular strategies
5. Guides to the strategies that will improve the candidate's standing among each category of voters.[16]

Although this information stands as the rewards for effective polling and analysis, it is not easy to obtain. Certain problems with the personnel who do the polling, and certain problems with even the best-run poll make it unlikely that party leaders will develop routines that insure the maximum exploitation of opinion surveys.

One of the most obvious deterrants to effective polling is its cost. In order to administer a survey that will produce findings that are representative of the electorate, it is necessary to hire technicians who can write unbiased questions and draw a representative sample, and interviewers who will contact the appropriate respondents and present questions in the proper manner. In the face of these expenses, party leaders must fight off their colleagues who claim that their own intuitive assessments of public opinion are superior to the results of professional pollsters, or who recommend less expensive means of polling the electorate. A number of candidates substitute mass-mail polls for the more expensive interviews, sometimes with disastrous results. When the rate of returned questionnaires falls to 8–10 percent, and when these returns come from a biased (or, even worse, an unknown) segment of the public, the candidate may be led astray by unrepresentative findings.[17] We saw above the folly that can occur when a candidate accepts the findings of an untrained observer. The intuitive politician in Massachusetts overestimated his candidate's support by 63 percent, and predicted the outcome correctly in only one of seven major cities.

Even after an accurate poll is taken, there are problems in making its findings relevant for the campaign. If the analysts are more dedicated to flattering the candidate than to honesty, they may cover up negative findings or exaggerate positive findings in ways that prevent a necessary change in the campaign. Ambiguous findings can be made oversimple, and minor differences between the attitudes of different groups can be magnified beyond any statistical justification. Even where evaluations are made honestly, the complexity of findings can retard their translation into effective tactics. Where the results indicate that a certain approach may increase the candidate's appeal to one group in his coalition but increase his problems with others, science is no longer helpful. "Art" and "judgment" must take over in ways that do not lend themselves to routine application.

The campaigner's problems with the media of radio, television, and newspapers concern the predictability of their impact on the electorate, the design of advertisements, and the news and editorial policies that are followed by owners of the media. There are few general principles about voter responsiveness to political messages that are helpful in a particular campaign. The phenomenon of selective perception (readers tend to notice those messages

which reinforce established prejudices) and the avoidance by
many citizens of political news and editorials lessen the influence
of the mass media. Yet the circumstances in any one community
may increase or diminish the importance of the media for an
election.

One of the problems with the mass media stems from the lack
of party discipline. Because many candidates cannot count on the
loyalty of party workers or voters, they must decide whether to
use the media to communicate with their party workers or the
voters. The obvious choice is to appeal to both, but it may be
necessary to decide about emphasis. The style of appeal that
would maximize the efforts of party workers might have a different effect on certain voters. Where the party workers need further
stimulus, the prescription may call for a reaffirmation of historic
party ideologies. In the case of the Republican Party, however, it
would be dangerous to make this appeal to the entire electorate.
It would alienate independents and marginal Democrats who
might have supported a bland Republican. In 1964 Barry Goldwater directed a type of campaign to the public which should
have been restricted to party workers. The reaffirmation of traditional symbols (financial conservatism and restricted government
services) may have whipped some partisans to fever pitch, but
also dampened public appeal.

4. The candidates

Candidates for elective office are neither machine-made to a
common mold nor pliable in the light of strategic demands. They
vary in their personality traits, their oratorical and intellectual
skills, and their willingness to follow the advice of staff assistants.
This variety in the candidate factor is yet another phenomenon
that hinders the routinization of party activities.

No matter how much a public relations firm can do for the
"packaging" of a candidate, there remains a wide range of important functions that he must carry off by himself. He must
maintain the loyalty and enthusiasm of his supporters, meet with
political "leaders" who influence convention delegates or voters,
and appear in public and on television. Each performance can be
more or less successful on account of the candidate's appearance,
the tone of his voice, his ability to grasp and deal with the subject

at issue, and his style of presentation. If a candidate scores low on some of these points, he may or may not be willing or able to alter his presentation at the behest of advisors.

A candidate can also be an asset (or a liability) because of his skill in assessing and planning his own strategy. The most desirable candidates have an intimate knowledge of the electorate, an accurate understanding of their own assets and weaknesses, and an inventive mind that will reinforce the efforts of his strategists. At the opposite extreme is the insecure campaigner who insists on pitching his appeal to his own inadequate self-image, who projects to his advisors a strong personal need for security (which encourages them to bias their assessments in the direction of flattery), and whose strategic vocabulary is heavily laden with cliches.

Candidates also vary in the values which they employ in deciding whether a particular tactic is "fair" or "acceptable." Many campaigns raise choices about the candidates' willingness to attack their opponents, the inclusion of invective or ridicule in the attack, and the introduction of ethnic, religious, or racial symbols. The standards of the candidate enter the translation of survey data into strategy and tactics. These standards are not uniform among candidates, and their variability provides one additional hindrance to the development of campaign routines.

Finally, candidates vary in their desire to lead or follow public opinion. They range in posture between the Burkean and the populist. Their choice of role may influence their decision to use public opinion polls or to revise their campaign in light of the results. While a Burkean might shun findings that suggest a change in platform, a populist might rewrite his own views. Although the relative success of the Burkean or populist would likely depend upon other factors, their differences in flexibility might affect their party's use of professional analysts and advisors.

ARE AMERICAN PARTIES PECULIAR WITH RESPECT TO ROUTINES?

Until now we have focused on American parties. Our basic argument has been that variations in the electorate, the party structure, the problems inherent in campaign media, and the candidates inhibit party leaders from developing and sharing routine decision processes. Much of our argument has rested on the undisciplined nature of American voters and party leaders. Thus, the reader might be inclined to believe that our projected result (the sparse development of party routines) is a peculiarly American phenomenon, reflecting the loose structure of each major party.

A rigorous cross-national analysis might find that American parties have developed fewer routines than counterparts elsewhere. However, one study of British campaigning suggests that many of the factors that discourage the development of routines here also work there—despite the reputation of British parties for greater integration and discipline.[18] The British electorate is heterogeneous (although perhaps less so than our own), and its voters are subject to cross-pressures from different loyalties. Hence, party leaders have no easy way to predict the impact of alternative strategies. Although British parties are not divided in ways that are as sharp as the state-national divisions that bother American parties, the British do experience conflicts between different party organs. In the Conservative Party there are sometimes sharp disagreements between the candidates and personnel in the Central Office. In the Labour Party there are policy and strategic differences between leaders of the Parliamentary Party and officers of the trade unions. As in the United States, intraparty conflicts must be taken into account by those who plan the campaigns, and they mar the smooth transition from information obtained about the electorate, to the planning and administration of a campaign. Also in Britain, party workers vary greatly in their attitude toward public opinion polling. Candidates also vary in their campaigning skills, in the tactics they are willing to use, and in their view of themselves as leaders or followers of public opinion. It appears that the routinization of British campaigning has not proceeded far.

The chief conclusion that can be drawn from this study of electoral propaganda is that the rational, vote-maximizing politician, acting with consistency and empirical justification in pursuit of a single electoral goal, is a myth. Campaigners are only imperfectly and intermittently rational. The lack of consistency in behavior—between campaigners and within a single campaign—is evidence by differences in values, sources of information about voters, timing, financing, and choice of subjects and styles for propaganda messages.[19]

The numerous factors that hinder the development of routinized party activity do not mean that party leaders pursue their
craft in a totally unpatterned manner. There are principles which
govern the response of leaders to various campaign situations.
These principles differ from routines, however, on several dimensions. They are not as precise as routines in the activity which
they prescribe, and they are not widely shared among decision-
makers in numerous party organizations. In the hierarchy of
decision-making aids that individuals use, *principles* stand lower
than *routines*. Principles are acquired by fledgling politicians as
they learn the vocabulary of the trade. But they do not become
deeply-ingrained reflexes of the professional politician. Partly because amateurs make many of the important campaign decisions,
and partly because the nature of the decision-situation is marked
by widely varying and unpredictable phenomena, the principles
that we discuss below seem to be irrelevant for most decisions of
party leaders.[20]

As we describe some principles of party behavior, it will prove
helpful to divide them into principles of grand strategy and principles of tactics. As the terms imply, those in the first classification
purport to guide basic decisions. Principles in the second classification are more specific in their application to limited phases of
the campaign. In both cases, however, the principles lack the
precision or the wide acceptance that was described for the
routines in Chapters III–VII.

Principles of grand strategy

Some principles of grand strategy are defined in a way that
makes them relevant for all types of candidates. Others are more
limited in their application. Some pertain to the front runner or
the under dog, some to the incumbent or the challenger, and some
to Republicans or Democrats.

One of the principles that is relevant for all types of campaigners is the advice to focus campaign efforts on the marginal voters,
instead of those who are clearly committed or opposed. In some
campaigns there are additional principles which may be relevant
to this point. Where sharp ethnic or religious cleavages play an
important role in determining voter choices, then one principle

would urge the candidate to expect support from his co-ethnics or his co-religionists, and to focus his efforts in those who are ethnically neutral. The problem with this advice is that it leaves many crucial decisions unmade. A candidate still must decide about the strategy to use in attracting support from marginal voters. Strategies that are directed at marginal groups might disturb some of his "most firm" admirers. Some supporters may need reinforcement during the campaign—either to insure their turnout at the polls, or to prompt their own efforts in proselytizing among marginal voters. The principle about co-ethnics and co-religionists does not take into account conflicts within ethnic or religious groups. Depending on the cleavages and the partisanship that is aroused by the issues of the current campaign, a candidate may receive more or less support from his own cultural group. His use of ethnic or religious symbols might add to the support from his own group, but (again depending upon circumstances) they might lose him the support of individuals who identify with other groups.

Another set of principles suggests alternative strategies to those mentioned above. Unfortunately they do not clarify which should be used under what conditions. One principle urges party leaders to maintain doctrinal differences between their own party and their opponent. Presumably, each should continue a tradition that can be identified by citizens and used to cement their loyalty and guide their votes. This principle has some appeal, but it requires a choice between issue-flexibility in order to appeal to marginal voters, or issue-consistency in order to maintain one's party traditions. The contrary principles suggest parameters within which candidates should operate: some flexibility to attract marginal voters; but some constancy with past traditions. The degrees of response to each principle will vary, presumably, with the circumstances of the campaign as they are viewed by the candidate and his advisors.

One principle that pertains solely to the candidate who considers himself the front runner advises that he does not alienate the opposition. Expressed in simpler terms, this principle states that the leader should leave well-enough alone, and concentrate his efforts in maintaining the support (presumably sufficient for victory) that he already has. Of course, the prior problem is to be certain of enough votes for victory, and to keep up with this information as factors external to the campaign may alter the loyalties of certain voters. This principle seems to apply only in campaigns that are relatively uncompetitive. Such campaigns may be declining in number, and where they continue the long-tenured incumbents may have little need for guidance.

A principle for the party in power advises it to renominate officeholders who want to succeed themselves. The failure to renominate may invite an intraparty hassle that will advertise organizational weaknesses, acerbate internal tensions, and invite disaster in the general election. It is assumed that incumbents (especially chief executives) have certain advantages which come from publicity given to their office, and from their control over patronage. Although the principle to "renominate incumbents" provides a clear prescription, it has limited application in elections for major office. The 22nd Amendment of the United States Constitution insures that it will apply to no more than one-half of the presidential elections, and the laws of 23 state governments limit the governor's ability to succeed himself. Moreover, the principle offers little guidance beyond the decision to renominate. It leaves open all of the questions of campaign strategy that we have discussed before, and provides no help in those cases when the incumbent's appeal appears shaky.

Several principles offer guidance to the candidates of one party: Republicans should make a bipartisan appeal during the general election campaign, emphasize international issues in presidential campaigns, and de-emphasize domestic issues; Democrats should stress party traditions during the general election, emphasize domestic issues, and play down international issues. These principles reflect the differential electoral base of each party, and the image which each has in political folklore. The Republicans earned an unfavorable reputation for domestic policy when the Hoover administration coincided with the onset of the Depression. The Democrats have been hurt by their tenure during World War I, World War II, the Korean Conflict, and Viet Nam. These principles must be judged in the light of others which recommend maintaining the distinctiveness of the parties, or pitching one's appeal broadly in order to attract members of the opposite party. And all principles may be outweighed by present circumstances. During 1964, for example, President Johnson was advised to emphasize his own foreign policy despite the country's growing involvement in Viet Nam, because his Republican opponent was voicing an even more aggressive posture on the conflict.

Principles of tactics

Tactical principles are generally narrow in their application to certain phases of the campaign, and sometimes to specific instances. They have the look of strict precision, but in leaving out reference to contingencies that may govern the situation, each is severely limited in its utility.

One tactical principle urges the presidential nominee of the Republican Party to repudiate conservative Congressmen from his own party.[21] This, presumably, will increase his appeal to the marginal voters, but it might also diminish the campaign enthusiasm of habitual partisans, and thereby reduce the party's total vote. Another principle urges presidential nominees to balance their own characteristics with their selection of a running mate.[22] If a liberal Republican (perhaps chosen by party leaders responding to the first principle) were to accept such advice, he would have to ignore the first principle and choose a conservative running mate.

Several principles pertain to the pre-convention and convention behavior of presidential contenders.[23] One advises candidates to enter only those primaries they expect to win! A loss in any primary would create a major obstacle, since it testifies to the weakness of the defeated candidate. But few candidates can be certain of success—or failure—in a contest. Serious controversies rage over the usefulness of survey research and the problems in extrapolating from its findings to a forecast. Also, candidates defeated in individual primaries have gone on to win the nomination.

Once the convention is in progress, the bandwagon principle urges delegates to support a candidate who appears headed for victory. This principle rests on the assumption that post-election goodies will come to those who recorded their support early for the winning candidate. A corollary of this principle advises delegates to give up their support of a candidate when his total vote reaches a plateau short of the nomination. Someone else will be nominated, and a delegate should find an early seat on the victor's bandwagon.

Another principle urges convention delegates to nominate a candidate who can win the election, unify the national party, and strengthen individual state parties. Where no one contender scores highest on each of these points, a judicious combination of presidential and vice-presidential nominations may provide the major needs in a balanced way. Insofar as this principle is considered along with the principle of the bandwagon, however, the delegate's view of each candidate's immediate prospects will be crucial in determining the rule that he actually follows.

One additional principle for the convention urges the candidate not to rely on the last-minute conversion of delegates. Convention strength comes to those who invest long months in wooing the leaders of state delegations. But like all the other principles covered in this chapter, this one does not promise success to the candidate who accepts the advice. Many factors beside long and careful wooing go into the convention's decision. Among the factors involved are many of the features discussed in the first section of this chapter. Delegates take into account the mood of the electorate as they perceive it, the structure of the party organization and intraparty conflicts, public opinion polls, each candidate's support from the press, and perhaps more than anything their own feelings of how the candidates' images, styles, and convictions will impress the voters. As we have argued throughout this chapter, the complexity of the decision situation—as well as the nonprofessional nature of many party actors—restricts the development of routines that can be used by most party leaders in making important decisions.

SUMMARY AND CONCLUSIONS

Many features in the character and environment of political parties lessen the predictability of certain behaviors and create an instability that frustrates routine decision-making. These features exist in the characteristics of the electorate, in the party organizations and candidates, and in the media which are used to learn about voters' attitudes and transmit information about the candidates to the voters. The inability of party leaders to count on disciplined subordinates or voters is central to the lack of widely shared routines. Loyalties may shift under the influence of issues, personalities, or styles in a campaign. The complex and overlapping identifications of party *supporters* make it difficult to predict which combination of circumstances will serve to weaken or reinforce party ties. The nondoctrinaire nature of the parties leads candidates to make ambiguous appeals in the hope of winning voters of different ideological persuasions. This helps to insure that "style" considerations will weigh heavily in a campaign. In a style campaign it is even more difficult than usual to assess each party's effort and to prescribe mid-campaign alterations. The lack of party discipline is especially evident in intraparty disputes between candidates for national office and candidates for state offices. The party structures are fractured along the lines of the federal system, and intense national-state jealousies preclude the establishment of well financed, professionally staffed central offices. Without well staffed and financed central offices, the parties may continue to suffer under the weight of a complex environment without well tested devices to simplify the considerations that are used in decision-making. The candidates themselves provide further problems that stand in the way of routinized campaigns. Candidates differ in the extent to which their personal style and physical condition will meet the requirements of their advisors' prescriptions.

A manifestation of weak party discipline is the lack of professional staffs that can develop routine decision rules and transmit them to later generations of decision-makers. A large number of the people who make decisions during campaigns are amateur politicians who spend less than full time on their job, who have not benefited from an orderly process of "professional" training or apprenticeship, and who consequently make their decisions without a systematic knowledge of other possible decisions and their likely outcomes. Party "machines" and other state and local party organizations are exceptions to this general rule of amateurism, but they seem to have developed no decision-rules that have been generally accepted by party organizations across the nation. Parties lack decision-rules that are in prominent use among their leaders. As we saw above in Chapter III–VII, this contrasts with the routines that are widespread among individual voters, budget-makers, legislatures, and certain other policy-makers in federal, state, or local agencies.

The decisions of political party leaders are not entirely unpatterned. Several principles of grand strategy and tactics are mentioned frequently in the literature. Compared to routines, however, these principles are less useful as rules of decision-making. Principles are not widely shared by party officials. Many lack sufficient precision to guide decision-makers, while others are so specific with respect to the phase or type of campaign that they have limited usefulness. Many principles show no regard for contingencies that would have to be considered in implementing campaign advice. And finally, some principles seem to contradict one another, and they give no indication which the decision-maker should choose.

NOTES

1. Frank J. Sorauf, *Party Politics in America* (Boston: Little, Brown, 1968), p. 58.

2. Murray B. Levin, *The Complete Politician: Political Strategy in Massachusetts* (Indianapolis: Bobbs-Merrill, 1962), pp. 179–80.

3. Angus Campbell, Philip E. Converse, Warren E. Miller and Donald E. Stokes, *The American Voter* (New York: John P. Wiley, 1960), p. 249.

4. Levin, *op. cit.,* pp. 153–54.

5. *Ibid.,* p. 167.

6. *Ibid.,* p. 168.

7. Richard Rose, *Influencing Voters: A Study of Campaign Rationality* (New York: St. Martin's Press, 1967), p. 189.

8. Alexander Heard, *The Costs of Democracy: Financing American Political Campaigns* (Garden City: Anchor Books, 1962), pp. 255 ff.

9. Anthony Downs, *An Economic Theory of Democracy* (New York: Harper, 1957), Chapter 8.

10. Sorauf, *op. cit.,* p. 127.

11. Levin, *op. cit.,* p. 184.

12. Rose reports some instances where personal ties affected candidate's choices of key campaign aides. On one occasion during a presidential campaign, personal relations seemed responsible for the shift in the public relations firm that was employed by the candidate. *op. cit.,* p. 242.

13. Sorauf, *op. cit.,* p. 68.

14. *Ibid.,* p. 39.

15. Samuel J. Eldersveld, *Political Parties: A Behavioral Analysis* (Chicago: Rand McNally, 1964), p. 340.

16. Levin, *op. cit.,* pp. 192–93.

17. *Ibid.,* p. 188.

18. Rose, *op. cit.;* it is possible that a study of the highly bureaucratized European Communist Parties will discover routines that are not found in the amateurish American parties.

19. *Ibid.,* pp. 194–95.

20. The principles reported below have been culled from the works of Levin, Rose, Heard, Downs, that we cited above, and from Nelson W.

Polsby and Aaron B. Wildavsky, *Presidential Elections: Strategies of American Electoral Politics* (New York: Scribners, 1964).

21. Polsby and Wildavsky, *op. cit.*, p. 115.

22. *Ibid.*, p. 92.

23. The priniciples pertaining to convention tactics are found succinctly in Nelson W. Polsby and Aaron B. Wildavsky, "Uncertainty and Decision-Making at the National Conventions," in Nelson W. Polsby, Robert A. Dentler, and Paul A. Smith, *Politics and Social Life: An Introduction to Political Behavior* (Boston: Houghton Mifflin Company, 1963), pp. 370–89.

IX. Interest Groups: More Organization Without Routines

THIS IS THE SECOND CHAPTER THAT EXPLAINS CONDITIONS UNDER which routines are *unlikely* to develop. Its subject matter is the interest group, one of the phenomena that is typically included in any political scientist's discussion about American politics and policy-making. In many of these descriptions, the interest groups are coupled with political parties as media which citizens and elites use in order to influence the composition of government or the ingredients of policy. Although parties are more inclusive in their memberships than interest groups, parties in the United States are not sufficiently doctrinaire to preempt the role of intermediary between individuals and public policy. Interest groups may work through parties, and seek to influence the ingredients of policy by first influencing the persons elected to the legislature or the executive. Or they may work directly on legislators, executives, administrators, or judicial officers, without committing themselves to the electoral support of one party's candidates.

The factors which retard the development of routines in interest groups resemble the factors discussed in the chapter on parties. These include a large number of participants, a lack of professional training or orderly apprenticeships in the preparation of interest group officials, a variety among interest groups that make it unlikely they will share decision rules with one another, and complex decision situations. Many of the decisions made by interest groups concern strategies that will be pursued in negotiations with parties, government officials, or other interest groups. The nature of these strategic decisions is such that even under the best of conditions—with personnel of long tenure and professional training—the circumstances would not lend themselves to routinized decisions.

Also as in parties, the decision-rules cited by interest group officials tend to be principles instead of routines. These principles lack the precision and wide acceptance which characterizes

routines. They tend to be vague, limited in the circumstances that
they cover, contradictory with respect to other principles, and
devoid of guidelines to help decision-makers choose the right
principle in a given context.

FACTORS INHIBITING THE DEVELOPMENT OF INTEREST GROUP ROUTINES

In this section we discuss several phenomena that seem to
hinder the development of routine decision-processes among the
officials of interest groups: (1) characteristics of the American
political system; (2) characteristics of interest groups; (3) characteristics of the institutions that are the targets of interest group
strategy; and (4) situational characteristics that are found in group-
government relationships.

1. The American political system

When we think of an "American political system" in relation to
interest group routines, we have in mind an imposing body of
institutions, actors, formal regulations, and traditions. It is obvi-
ously not all of this which hinders the routinization of decisions.
Among the features of the political system, these which seem to
be most important for decision-making within interest groups are
the status of interest groups amidst other institutions and actors in
the system, and the impact on interest groups from the constitutional separation of powers—checks and balances.

The status of interest groups is made legitimate by that section
of the first amendment to the Constitution which guarantees that
"Congress shall make no law respecting . . . the right of the
people peaceably to assemble, and to petition the Government for
a redress of grievances." Much of the activity that groups pursue
is not, strictly speaking, concerned with seeking a redress of
grievances. Groups seek to *forestall grievances that they predict
for their future* by obtaining rulings against certain forms of
public or private behaviors. And they seek *positive advantages* by
obtaining decisions that provide their members with public services tailored to their desires.

The status of interest groups rests on the footing of cooperative
arrangements made with government officials, as well as on the
formal basis of constitutional guarantee. Legislators, executives,

and administrators see benefits for themselves in the information which interest groups provide. This information includes statements about the policy preferences of group leaders and factual data pertaining to the social or economic conditions which make certain policy changes desirable. A knowledge of preferences helps government officials to assess the political implications of their decisions, and the factual data may help them justify their own decisions. By supplying credible information, interest groups can supplement the government's own research facilities.

Although the status of interest groups receives support from both law and custom, their status is not uniformly one of respect and trust. Intermingled in their image is that of the selfish lobbyist who would satisfy his group's private interest at the expense of the public. The history of lobbying includes episodes of deceit on the part of lobbyists, heavily-financed campaigns designed to cause the defeat of elected officials, and overt attempts to bribe government officials. Decision-makers are sensitive to this aspect of interest group tradition. If they perceive *undesirable pressures* coming from interest groups, they are capable of closing communication and frustrating a group's desire to influence policy.

The ambiguity of the interest group's status has a bearing on the routinization of decision-making. Although most groups can expect a fair hearing from government officials—and plan their strategy accordingly—the negative aspects of their status caution them that an unwise move may result in the termination of their contact. The particular type of communication that will prove offensive varies from one public official to another, and may reflect their experience with "offensive" interest groups. The ability of a government official to terminate relations with interest groups appears inconsistent with the reputed status of groups as the dominant actors in the interest-government relationship, and calls into question the *group interpretation* of politics. However, the secondary position of the interest group is something which the lobbyists themselves admit. In response to a question about the relative influence of various actors in policy-making, more than one-half of 114 lobbyists surveyed in one study named the President or the executive branch as the most important participant, about 20 percent named the voters as most important, 10 percent named Congress, and only one of the respondents gave first rank to lobbyists.[1] In concluding another study of interest group activities in Congress, two authors made their evaluation of the status of interest groups, and the group interpretation of politics:

The group interpretation of legislative behavior offers an elite theory of government. Like most elite theories, it places heavy demands on the alleged elite. Unfortunately for the theory, interest groups cannot live up to their billing; they simply do not have the instruments of power at their disposal . . .

The congressman tends to believe that interest groups exist, as far as he is concerned, to perform certain service functions that are primarily information-related. He feels that he is not much more obligated to a group when he avails himself of its information facilities than he would be to the information clerk at the National Airport . . . . legislative action is *not* simply the vector of interest group pressures on Congress.[2]

The legislature does not present a clean slate upon which interest groups can write policy. The legislature—and other organs of government—are dynamic institutions, filled with persons who live according to a variety of personal and institutional norms. They have their own desires for public policy, and these desires are among the most formidable barriers to the routinization of tactics on the part of lobbyists. Groups must plan their actions in the light of a prior assessment about what government officials are likely to demand in the decision-situation.

The constitutional provisions of separated powers and checks and balances affect the needs of government officials and complicate the assessment of these needs by interest groups. No single congressional committee or administrative agency can prevail in policy-making without taking into consideration the interests of other institutions in the federal government and—if it is a matter involving intergovernmental relations—state and local governments. If it is the purpose of a group to prevent the implementation of a new policy, then the separation of powers and checks and balances simplifies its task. It need obtain the support of only one institution among several that can block new action with a negative decision. If the interest group wishes to insert a provision into public policy, however, then the need for agreement among numerous units of government complicates its task. It must reckon with the policy inclinations of several institutions—perhaps at several levels of government—and their sentiments toward one another that might color relationships on the matter at issue. These computations are sufficiently complex so that interest group decisions about strategy are not likely to be made according to any simple routines.

2. Characteristics of interest groups

The variation among interest groups is one of the characteristics that limits the development of routine decision-rules. The *resources* of interest groups vary on the dimensions of membership size, wealth, social status, political cohesion, the intensity with which members pursue group goals, and the respect that they enjoy in government circles. These ingredients help determine the likelihood of a group's success. Because of variations in these resources from one group to another, it is unlikely that decision-rules developed by any one group will have great relevance for many others.

Even where interest groups show a rough equivalence on the dimensions of resources, their differences in *goals* may make the experience of one group unimportant for another group. Two labor union locals of similar size, wealth, and community prestige may have different political needs that prompt their officers in different strategic directions. Craft unions (plumbers, electricians, masons) have a vital interest in the regulatory policies of local governments, and develop strategies that will maximize their access to local officials of either political party. The locals of industrial unions (auto workers, mine workers), in contrast, are more likely to take their political cues from national leaders. So they may try to build support among their members for candidates of a national party. Within the ranks of the industrial unions, however, there are differences in goals between those whose work agreements are settled nationally, and those which bargain over important issues in the local community. Where local negotiations are important, the unions may be less inclined to link themselves with either national party at the local level.[3]

Another trait which hinders the routinization of interest group decisions lies in their inability to count on the members' disciplined response to leaders' choice of strategy. Part of the problem results from "overlapping memberships." Each member identifies with several interests that occasionally make inconsistent demands. Although group leaders employ a variety of media (newspapers, radio, television, and personal appeals by activists) in an attempt to solidify their members behind certain positions, they usually fall short of uniformity within their own groups. One survey made during the 1952 presidential campaign found that only 29 percent of the respondents from blue-collar union families expressed agreement with the widely-publicized union position on repeal of the Taft-Hartley bill. Twelve percent of blue-collar union respondents expressed the anti-union position on the issue, and 41 percent failed to express an opinion.[4] Members' loyalty to group norms vary with their sense of group identification. As expected, the more closely the member identifies with the organization, the more he votes in accordance with its leadership's strategy. Even here, however, the members who consider themselves to be highly identified with the group may take positions different from the leaders' instructions. A survey taken during the 1956 campaign found that only 64 percent of respondents from union families who identified strongly with the union would vote for the Democratic candidate, while 36 percent of those who identified weakly with the union would vote Democratic.[5] One factor which adds to the cross-pressures felt by group members comes from the techniques of interest group leaders themselves. When leaders of different groups compete among themselves for organizing similar populations, they create alternatives for the members which may limit their own future success in building internal unity. There is competition among various spokesmen for labor, farmers, veterans, Negroes, Catholics, Jews, and businessmen.[6]

One of the factors which reduce a group's discipline on political matters is the feeling among members that the group should not express itself on political issues. Many individuals who are nominally members of an interest group joined the group without any thought about politics. Union members may have joined only because they had to as part of their job, and members of church groups that take political postures may have joined purely for religious reasons. A survey taken in 1956 found that only 49 percent of the people from union households felt it was "all right" for their union to take a stand in support of candidates.[7]

Another significant trait of interest groups is the absence of a career pattern that would provide for the systematic training or apprenticeship of leaders. Lobbyists come from a variety of backgrounds, each of which may provide them with some relevant preparation, but which fail to provide a consistent body of professional lore and practice. Table IX-1 shows the composition of lobbyists by previous position and professional training. No single category of career background or professional training accounts for as much as 40 percent of the lobbyists. Without a commonality of background, these individuals seem unlikely to develop any routines for decision-making out of their training or experience.

TABLE IX-1

Position Held Immediately Prior to Becoming a Lobbyist

Prior position	Number
Never did anything else	2
Lawyer	9
Journalist	1
Elective public official	3
Businessman	18
Government job-holder—executive branch	41
Government job-holder—legislative branch	16
Other professional	4
Labor union employee	5
Other	7
No response	8
	114

Source: Lester Milbrath, *The Washington Lobbyists* (Chicago: Rand McNally, 1963), p. 68.

3. Characteristics of target institutions

The prime targets of interest group activity are government institutions. Their decisions comprise public policy and create the situations that lobbyists hope to influence. Any consideration of the factors that affect the decision processes of interest groups must take account of these targets.

One feature of government institutions is their capacity to dominate relationships with interest groups.

Analysts of the political process often overlook the fact that the elected officials have the upper hand in setting up and enforcing the rules. This is especially true in the relationship between lobbyists and officials. Officials can make decisions without consulting or depending on anyone else—except the voters at the next election. They can neutralize the lobbyists by cutting off access or neglecting to listen. They have many alternative sources for the information they seek. Lobbyists have much less power; they can accomplish their ends only by reaching officials; they have no alternative target. It is the officials who admit the lobbyists to the trust relationship—not vice versa.[8]

Although the author of this statement overlooks the lobbyists' opportunity to apply his pressure to any of several officials, and perhaps to play some officials off against others, the general point is well taken. As we noted above in the discussion of the American political system, there are no single officials who can implement major policy decisions by themselves. The features of separation of powers and checks and balances requires cooperation among many officials for major new ventures. If a lobbyist desires to block all action on a proposal, he may be able to pick and choose among the officials he will contact. If the lobbyist wishes to have a positive impact on policy, however, he must earn the cooperation of many officials, any one of whom may shut off his access and frustrate his program.

Once we appreciate the capacity of government officials to dominate their relationships with interest groups, we can understand the importance of officials' attitudes and behaviors for the ways in which interest groups make their decisions. In the following paragraphs, we shall document several characteristics of government officials that make their responses to interest group strategies irregular and hard to predict. Because interest group leaders cannot comprehend with sufficient accuracy the response that any particular strategy will elicit from government officials, they are hard pressed to routinize their own decision processes.

One problem that lobbyists face in their relations with government concerns the officials' choice of their "roles" with respect to interest groups. Roles represent the officials' conception of proper behavior. The role-choices which are relevant to interest groups run the gamut from "facilitator" through "neutral" to "resistor"; these names suggest the quality of responsiveness to the needs and desires of interest groups.[9] These roles reflect historic alternatives in the postures that government officials have taken toward the public's wishes. At one pole lies the official who considers himself to be the representative of the public, with responsibility for discerning the *public's wishes* and seeking to implement these in the nature of policy. At the other pole is the position articulated by Edmund Burke; the elected official should use his abilities to determine *what policies his constituents should have.* Such an official would picture himself as a leader instead of a follower with respect to public opinion. Although both the "representative" and the "leader" might give a fair hearing to a lobbyist, the "leader" would be less inclined to accept a report about the public's desires (even if it were an accurate assessment of public opinion) as the prevailing criteria for his own decision.

Interest groups often cannot obtain a fair hearing of their case, even from facilitative officials. Interest groups suffer because of officials' "information overload," created by a surplus of individuals and groups who seek the attention of legislators and administrators.

It is physically impossible for any government official to attend to all the communications directed to him. Officials use their personal perceptual screen to protect themselves from some of this overload. They also have devised some institutional means, such as staff assistants and data coding, to help them sort, condense, and comprehend as much of the incoming information as possible. In the scramble for limited attention, the lobbyist must plan carefully and seize a rare moment of receptivity to drive home a communication.[10]

Some of the communications overload is evident at the formal hearings of congressional committees. Witnesses typically address a limited number of committee members, and even these may be distracted to some other business. The legislators might "read over" the fat volumes of transcript that report the hearings, but there is little assurance that an official will perceive a spoken or written message that is sent in his direction. With communications subject to the vagaries of the recipient and the situation, it is clearly difficult for interest groups to routinize their dealings with government officials.

Even after an interest group's communication is received, it must run the obstacle of the official's own set of decision criteria before it can have an impact on public policy. The elements which may be crucial for the decisions of any individual in government include his own personal convictions about the matter at hand; his view of his constituency's desires; his view of the intensity with which constituents will promote their point of view; the nature of the position, if any, which his party leadership has taken on the policy; the advice and information given by his professional staff; and the recommendations made by trusted colleagues. The desires of an interest group must compete with these alternate cues. Insofar as officials vary in the types of criteria they will value in making their decisions, lobbyists cannot be sure of what cues they must compete against.

4. Characteristics of the situation

A large number of factors condition the success which interest groups enjoy in influencing the nature of public policy. Indeed, the very number of these factors serves to lessen the capacity of lobbyists to identify the salient variables in their environment and to routinize their decisions. Interest groups must not only plan their strategy in a way to take account of numerous elements of the political system, their own resources, and characteristics of the target institution. Each decision situation presents a mix of these conditions. It is the mix—rather than discrete ingredients—which may prevail upon the decisions of government officials. At times, the contingencies envisioned are incredibly complex. An example is provided in the following prescription that is elaborated in full recognition of relevant contingencies:

Although collaboration (among interest groups seeking common goals) has many advantages, it is not adaptable to all situations and can be overrated as a general approach. It seems to work most effectively on specific bills or policies in which several organizations have a common interest which is central to the *raison d'etre* of the respective organizations. There seems to be an optimum level of problem generality suitable for collaboration; problems that are too specific or too general do not benefit as much. If the problem is general but confined to a single industry, the chances for success by a united front are very good; however, if a given industry appears to be asking for special consideration on a problem that is common to many industries, the chances are less good. A broad general policy that affects many kinds of groups is less likely to be advanced significantly by a united front because such policies generally attract strong opposing coalitions. And some policy proposals are so specific in application that a coalition would look unnatural and forced.[11]

We can cite numerous other examples of the need for interest groups to evaluate a strategy in the light of situational factors. A mass media campaign designed to persuade government officials by virtue of popular support for the lobbyist's position may fail if the issue is too technical for public comprehension, if interest group members are themselves divided on the issue, or if propaganda costs are too great for the group's resources.

One aspect of the decision situation that may affect group strategists is the level of "politicization" which surrounds an issue. To the extent that an issue is widely publicized and involved in prominent political discourse, it will arouse many cues that are directed at the officials from different sources. On such an occasion, the pleas of an interest group have the most competition. When there is limited interest in a matter, and when most of the communications are coming from a single group, its lobbyists may be able to employ a routine set of decision-rules. Since these "unpolitical" situations have seldom been the subject of careful analysis, we know very little about them.

PRINCIPLES OF INTEREST GROUPS

As in previous chapters, our claims about interest groups reflect an assessment of general tendencies rather than uniform patterns. The presence of numerous factors that discourage the adoption of important routines that are used by most interest groups does not signify that no groups operate with regularized decision-rules. Some interest groups may have achieved a relationship with government agencies that is sufficiently stable and well-defined to support the development of routines. The spokesmen for defense contractors may use routines in their dealings with the military services, and the spokesmen for regulated industries may have developed certain routines for their relations with regulatory commissions.[12] Moreover, the claim that most groups operate without common routines does not mean that their decisions are made in the absence of any rules. A series of decision-rules which we shall call *principles* appear in the literature about interest groups. Some principles are widely recognized by lobbyists, but their popularity is partly a function of their simplicity. They read like children's homilies, and are equally helpless in the face of a difficult problem. There may be several principles that offer contradictory advice, and they are unlikely to contain the guidelines for choosing among alternates. When it comes to making key decisions, the strategist cannot rely on these principles.

The following list contains some of the more prominent principles of interest group decision-making. It may reveal in itself some internal contradictions and unanswered questions.

1. Be pleasant and non-offensive; do not apply overt pressure; avoid all signs of bribery or threat.

2. Convince officials that it is important for them to listen.

3. Be well prepared and well informed; emphasize facts that support your case.

4. If you are not personally convinced of your group's case, do not make the presentation.

5. Solidify your own membership behind the group position before you begin a public campaign; a divided group can be a fatal embarrassment for your purpose.

6. Maintain the appearance of genuinely representing your members' views.

7. Be succinct, well-organized, and direct.

8. Know your targets; aim your communications at key people who will be able to convince their rank and file.

9. Assess the predispositions of your targets; do not appeal to decision-makers who are clear in their opposition to your case; appeal to the uncommitted and reinforce your supporters.

10. Develop and maintain "trusting" relationships with officials; maintain your credibility.

11. If you attempt a campaign of mailed and telegraphed appeals to officials, urge individuality upon your letter writers; avoid the appearance of an organized effort, unless your numbers are so large that any type of mass-mailed communication will impress the recipients with your strength.

12. Show that your own desires are identical with the best interests of the target officials' constituents.[13]

Some of these principles are too vague to qualify as helpful decision-rules. The statement that lobbyists should "convince an official that it is important for him to listen"[14] is a platitude that does not inform the lobbyist how he should attract an official's attention. Recall the officials' information overload and their receipt of stimuli from many actors besides interest groups. Once an official is tuned in to a lobbyist's proposal, a large part of the communications problem is already solved. A great deal of strategic planning may have to precede the effective communication, and the planning process receives no guidance from this simplistic principle.

The principle which urges lobbyists to "be pleasant and non-offensive"[15] also provides minimum assistance. If a lobbyist were to compare this principle with that which recommends a "sound, well-organized, and direct" presentation, he might have trouble running a campaign that did not run afoul of one of them. Neither principle provides any clues about its own borders.

Some of the principles assume a higher level of information on the part of lobbyists than they are likely to possess. One principle, for example, urges lobbyists to know the predispositions of their targets. Although it seems likely that experienced lobbyists will be familiar with the general posture toward an issue which is held by members of a key legislative committee, they may lack accurate information about legislators with whom they communicate only rarely. Even among the best-known of the legislators, an assessment of their general position may not inform a lobbyist about their response to a particular bill. An agreement "in principle" need not translate into support for—or even tolerance of—the technical provisions that find their way into the crucial legislation. Principle # 13 may assume too high a level of information about the interest group membership. Many lobbyists realize the folly in a direct-mail campaign that results in hundreds of identical communications being sent to Congressmen. It is assumed that such letters are ignored, on the belief that the senders are not sufficiently concerned about the issue to draft an original letter. It is also felt, however, that the shortcomings of identical letters are overlooked if the volume of mail is sufficiently large.[16] Here is the problem for the strategist: if his members' response is huge, he may get some positive effect from a campaign of uniform letters or telegrams; but if he misjudges the members' enthusiasm for the issue, a mediocre volume of uniform communications may produce more embarrassment than benefit for the interest group. In light of ambiguous membership support for key issues,[17] a strategist should be wary before assuming that he knows enough about his group to risk a mass mail campaign.

None of the principles listed above forbids implied threats or pressure. It seems clear from the literature that the communications of many interest groups—especially those which are large and well-financed—carry an implied threat or an unspoken ability to "make trouble." "Trouble" does not have to be an overt campaign directed at defeating an official at the polls. The withdrawal of campaign contributions, the failure to re-invite an official to address large gatherings of the group's members, or the inclusion of adverse commentary about the official in the group's newsletters might be enough to provide a group with some cooperation. The principles listed above do not advise strategists how to take advantage of such opportunities that are open to them, and how to reckon with the complex contingencies of the target officials' predispositions, the political resources of the officials, and the support of the group's own membership for any particular strategy. In contrast to the routines that prevail in other arenas, these principles do not identify which of the many decision criteria should receive priority in the interest group's decisions.

SUMMARY AND CONCLUSIONS

Routines do not appear prominently in the decision-making processes of interest groups. The elements that retard routinization resemble the factors which retard the use of routines in political parties. It is a very complex environment in which interest groups and parties make their decisions. Each has relationships with numerous public and private individuals and institutions whose behaviors are often irregular and difficult to predict. The leaders of interest groups and political parties also lack an orderly, formal preparation for their jobs. The combination of a complex and fluid environment, plus the absence of professional leadership imposes severe barriers to the kind of orderly, long-observed decision-making which may be necessary for the development of routines.

The specific barriers to the routinization of interest group decisions include the large number of government actors with which the groups must deal, and whose responses to the groups are made irregular by the officials' own involvements in the institutional relationships that have grown out of our constitutional separation of powers—checks and balances. Many officials have sufficient political power to control the relationship between interest groups and themselves. The ambivalent status of lobbyists—ranging between the legitimate and the offensive—leads officials to develop their own norms about proper group behavior, and to threaten an end to the interest group's access under certain conditions. Some officials consider themselves to be facilitators with respect to interest groups, but others are hostile. Some legislators view themselves as the followers of the public's wishes, while others feel they should lead the public—at least on certain matters of policy. This variety in officials' roles makes it unlikely that any given situation will clearly invite a routinized strategy from a group.

The large number and great variety among interest groups makes it unlikely that many of them will trade information in a way that would foster the development of routines. Groups vary on the dimensions of size, wealth, social and political status, in the cohesion and intensity of their members, and in the character of their goals. One group's experience is not likely to help the strategists of many other groups. Even if experiences were comparable, inter-group competition and the lack of a "professional" orientation among group leaders minimizes the chances for information-aggregation and the definition of which routines "work well" under certain conditions.

Although there are no routines which appear to be prominent in the decision rules of most interest groups, there are "principles" which may be widely recognized by lobbyists. Like the principles we described in the chapter on parties, however, these tend to be shallow homilies, without clear meaning for concrete situations. Some principles are vague, some appear to contradict one another, and few give any guidance as to which principle is relevant in a specific situation.

NOTES

1. Lester W. Milbrath, *The Washington Lobbyists* (Chicago: Rand McNally, 1963), pp. 351–52.

2. Andrew M. Scott and Margaret A. Hunt, *Congress and Lobbies: Image and Reality* (Chapel Hill: University of North Carolina Press, 1966), pp. 89, 91, 97.

3. Edward C. Banfield and James Q. Wilson, *City Politics* (Cambridge: Harvard University Press, 1965), pp. 277–80.

4. V. O. Key, *Public Opinion and American Democracy* (New York: Knopf, 1961), p. 509.

5. Angus Campbell, Philip E. Converse, Warren E. Miller, and Donald E. Stokes, *The American Voter* (New York: Wiley, 1960), p. 309.

6. Key, *op. cit.*, p. 520.

7. Abraham Holtzman, *Interest Groups and Lobbying* (New York: Macmillan, 1966), p. 36.

8. Milbrath, *op. cit.*, p. 288.

9. John C. Wahlke, Heinz Eulau, William Buchanan, and Leroy Fer-

guson, *The Legislative System* (New York: Wiley, 1962).

10. Milbrath, *op. cit.*, p. 210.

11. *Ibid.*, p. 171.

12. Murray Edelman, *Symbolic Uses of Politics* (Urbana: University of Illinois Press, 1964), Chapter 2.

13. These principles were culled from the works cited above of Milbrath, Scott and Hunt, and Holtzman, plus Harmon Zeigler, *Interest Groups in American Society* (Englewood Cliffs: Prentice Hall, 1964); and Donald Matthews, *U.S. Senators and Their World* (New York: Vintage Books, 1960), Chapter VIII.

14. Milbrath, *op. cit.*, p. 220.

15. *Loc. cit.*

16. Mathews, *op. cit.*, p. 194.

17. See Note 4 above.

X. Deviations from Routines

ROUTINES ARE STABILIZING FACTORS IN THE POLITICAL SYSTEM. We argued in Chapter I that routines fit into the conversion processes (the "black box") of political systems and help to maintain equilibrium among the components of the systems. In subsequent chapters, we have seen how several routines do provide stability: they represent decision-rules that actors tend to use from one context to the next. Because of the stability of these rules, the decisions of actors are predictable, at least within certain ranges that are inherent in each routine. Insofar as the routines prescribe fixed treatment of certain inputs (i.e., demands, supports, resources) by the decision-makers, the use of these routines produces a relationship between inputs and the outputs of policy that remains constant from one situation to the next.

Some routines are explicit in carrying over past decisions to the present. The routines that individual citizens employ in perpetuating party loyalties serve to import the voting alignments of a generation past into contemporary election campaigns. Budget-makers who use routines of incrementalism pay great respect to their own decisions of the recent past. The result is that each unit's level of expenditures—relative to other units—remains stable.

Even those routines that do not perpetuate past patterns in an overt fashion do operate in a way to assure continuity in the outcomes of policy. The tendency of legislators to rely on the executive's budget recommendations makes it likely that a governor can regulate the increments of growth in agency expenditures without having his decision undermined in the legislature. The tendency of state and local officials to consult with regional neighbors makes it likely that policies in each region will show some predictable differences from national standards. The popularity of the spending-service cliche makes it predictable that officials' perceived need for improvements in their agency's services will find its outlet in their request for additional funds. Frequently this request will precede a thoroughgoing analysis of service determinants, and the likely returns to be associated with added expenditures for each determinant.

Although routines bring stability and conservatism to political systems, they do not impose rigor mortis. In each of our preceding chapters, we have described the *tendencies* of routines to influence the nature of individual's decisions. We have not talked about fixed rules or inflexible procedures.

In this chapter we focus upon those instances when routines do not operate in their typical fashion. We shall not be content merely to state that routines do not operate, but we shall make an effort to identify the conditions under which routines are changed, abandoned, or laid aside for a short while. This chapter has two principal messages. It serves as a fitting caveat in a book about routines by pointing to some limitations in the central concept. And secondly, it highlights an analytic side payment that is provided by the concept of routines: once we know that a certain routine is widespread in politics, we know that there must be something special about the circumstances when the routine is not used. Thus, our concept of routines is useful in pointing to deviant —and typical—cases. It provides us with the opportunity to isolate for purposes of intensive analysis those occasions when relationships among principal actors and their stimuli work either normally or in an unusual manner.

PROMINENT DEVIATIONS FROM ROUTINES

There are several obvious indications that the routines identified in this book are not inflexible. The history of party alignments in presidential elections testifies to occasional changes in the loyalties of many voters. A brief examination of trends in government expenditure reveals that incrementalism has not prevented most governments from increasing their expenditures greatly over a period of years, and it has not prevented individual agencies from increasing their budgets at rates which far exceed the average. The discussion of executive-legislative budget relations identified the state of Nebraska—during the 1965–67 period—as exhibiting an extreme deviant case of the Legislature acting consistently at odds with the recommendations of the governor. Despite the persistence of regional norms in decision-making processes, it is evident that state and local government agencies in the South have increased their expenditures—and perhaps their levels of service—to points far closer to the national average than was the case a generation ago. And despite the temptations for officials to continue assuming a simplistic relationship between levels of spending and service, there is a strong and widespread movement among budget analysts to "rationalize" budget-making through the introduction of systems analysis, cost-benefit calculations, and "planning-programming budgeting." By examining some of these prominent deviations from our routines, we will provide the basis for a later assessment of the *types of conditions* that are likely to provoke such changes in decision rules.

1. Deviations from established party loyalties

There were prominent changes in the voting habits of many Americans during national elections in the late 1920s and early 1930s, in the 1946 congressional election, and in 1952. The first change produced a lasting alteration in the composition of elective offices, while the later changes were temporary aberrations from entrenched patterns. The data which signal these deviations are displayed in Table X-1; they show the total number of voters participating, and the percentage cast for each major party during elections for President and U.S. Representative since 1900.

Perhaps the greatest electoral change in recent history is that which occurred between the presidential elections of 1924 and 1932. While the Democratic candidate in 1924 (the all-but-forgotten John W. Davis) polled a mere 28.8 percent of the vote, Franklin Roosevelt received 57.4 percent in 1932, and increased this to 60.8 percent in 1936. The lasting nature of this change is evident in the facts that only one Republican reached the Presidency between 1932 and 1967, and that the Republicans were able to gain control of Congress only during 1947–48 and 1953–54. Although it is common to associate the Democratic swing with the Depression and the candidacy of Roosevelt, the data suggest a movement away from Republican dominance as early as 1928. Al Smith received 40.8 percent of the vote in 1928, making him the most attractive Democratic candidate since Woodrow Wilson. If his campaign had not suffered under anti-Catholicism—especially in the normally Democratic states of the

TABLE X-1
Instances of Stability and Change in Voter Turnout and Competition:
National Elections 1900–1966*

	Vote cast (x1,000)	Percent Democratic	Percent Republican
1966	52,900	50.9	48.3
1964	70,645	61.1	38.5
1962	51,261	52.5	47.2
1960	68,836	49.7	49.5
1958	45,819	56.1	43.5
1956	62,015	42.0	57.4
1954	42,580	52.5	47.0
1952	61,303	44.5	55.2
1950	40,354	49.0	49.0
1948	48,691	49.5	45.1
1946	34,398	44.2	53.5
1944	47,969	53.4	45.9
1942	28,074	46.1	50.6
1940	49,891	54.7	44.7
1938	36,236	48.6	47.0
1936	45,643	60.8	36.5
1934	32,256	53.9	42.0
1932	39,732	57.4	39.7
1930	24,777	44.6	52.6
1928	36,812	40.8	58.1
1926	20,435	40.5	57.0
1924	29,086	28.8	54.0
1920	26,748	34.1	60.4
1916	18,531	49.3	46.1
1912	15,037	41.9	23.2
1908	14,884	43.1	51.6
1904	13,512	37.6	56.4
1900	13,368	45.5	51.7

*Data pertains to Presidential elections where they are held, and elections for U.S. Representatives in off-years.
Source: *Statistical Abstract of the United States, 1967*
            (Washington: U.S. Bureau of the Census).

South—he might have been the figure who broke the hold of the Republican Party on the majority of American voters.

It is an oversimplification to identify the Depression as the sole reason for the Democrats' acquisition of majority party status. Another phenomenon that occurred at the same time was the coming into politics of many individuals who had earlier remained away from the polls. Table X-1 shows that the total popular vote in presidential elections increased by almost 8 million between 1924 and 1928, and then by an additional 9 million by 1936. Many new voters were members of ethnic groups that immigrated to the United States after 1880. They first entered politics before the Depression, and they voted disproportionately for Al Smith. In part, this vote may have represented the emotional attraction of a Catholic candidate for Catholic voters. But more basically, the immigrants' support of Smith reflected the effort made by Democratic organizations in many states to solicit these new voters. The Democratic Party nominated ethnics to places on state and local ballots, and provided the traditional welfare services of the old-style political machines.[1] The Depression probably reinforced the feeling of alienation between the economically insecure ethnics and the middle- and upper-class Republicans, and added to the appeal of Roosevelt's campaign.

The aberrations in party loyalties of 1946, 1952 and 1968 seemed to be temporary reactions against wars and their effects upon the domestic scene. The election of 1946 was the first occasion after the fighting was over for American voters to express their disapproval of rationing, price and wage controls, and the dislocations associated with demobilization. The dominant party in Britain experienced a similar defeat in 1945, when the Conservatives lost to Labour. Despite Churchill's popular identification with the heroic defense of the homeland, the costs as well as the victories of war were associated with his party. The American election of 1952 occurred during a war which appeared to be stalemated, and the Republican candidate combined the attractions of a clean broom, a military expert, and a national hero. The war-time election for the House of Representatives in 1942 was likewise a defeat in popular vote for the Democrats, but they won enough districts to retain control of the House. Richard Nixon's narrow victory in 1968 owed something to the Viet Nam war, and its influence upon internal dissonance within the Democratic Party.

2. Deviations from incremental budgeting

Despite the reluctance of budgeteers to permit major increases, there have been tremendous increases in the level of government spending within the United States. Between 1932 and 1962, the aggregate of federal, state, and local government spending increased by 1,424 percent! There have also been great differences between the expenditure increases enjoyed by individual agencies. During the 1949–63 period, the appropriations for the entire federal government increased by about 100 percent. At the same time, however, the appropriation for the Office of Education increased by 2,562 percent.[2] There are also wide variations among state governments in their rates of expenditure change. During 1929–39, in particular, there were great differences in the states' response to the economic and social conditions. Total per capita expenditures in Arkansas increased during that period at only 42 percent of the nation-wide rate, while per capita expenditures in California increased at 166 percent of the nation-wide rate.[3] During the recent, more stable period of 1957–62, the range of variation was also great. Florida's per capita expenditures increased at only 76 percent of the nation-wide rate, while Kentucky's increased at 149 percent of that rate. If we were to look within state government budgets at the variations from one field of service to the next, we would also find considerable differences between the rates of expenditure change. It may be true that incrementalism is a phenomenon that is generally present in government budgeting, but it does not work the same at all times and in all places. Incrementalism is not the only force at work in budget-making.

Not all changes in expenditure reflect the weakness of the incremental routines. Many changes in spending are defended as special cases that are made necessary by increases in population and the resulting increase in the service loads of administrative agencies. Inflation also imposes some automatic decisions on budget-makers, who must increase the number of dollars in order to keep the same economic resources flowing through their agencies Table X-2 compares the change in total government spending over the 1932–62 period with the change in spending corrected for population and inflation. After these corrections are made, the magnitude of expenditure-change is only 259 percent, instead of the 1424 percent that appears with the uncorrected data. We can view this 259 percent change as the magnitude of resources being spent in 1962 beyond the levels of 1932. Much of

TABLE X-2

Changes in the Aggregate of Federal, State and Local Expenditure
1932–62, by Various Standards of Measurement

	1932	1962	Percent change
Total expenditures (x$1,000,000)	$12.437	$176.720	+1,424
Expenditures for domestic functions financed in common by federal, state and local govts.	8.700	79.300	811
Total expenditures per capita in constant dollars	238.50	618.00	259
Total common function expenditures per capita on constant (1954) dollars	177.18	329.28	86

Source: *Historical Statistics on Government Finances and Employment* (U.S. Bureau of the Census: Census of Governments, 1962).

this increase in real government spending has occurred in federal spending for military and international activities. We can estimate the weight of this factor by looking at the 1932–62 change in per capita constant dollar expenditures for the domestic functions which receive some of their financial support from federal, state and local governments. That change was only 86 percent—from $177.18 to $329.28.

3. Legislators who do not accept the executive's budget recommendations

Not all Congressmen or state legislators have surrendered control over the public treasury to their chief executive. Several Presidents have had to cope with the budget-cutting habits of Representatives Otto Passman and John Rooney; and Representative John Fogarty was labeled the "Santa Claus" of the Appropriations Committee for his willingness to provide *more* funds to an agency than had been requested by the President.

Governors Morrison of Nebraska and Reynolds of Wisconsin both found their legislatures unwilling to accept the executive's budget recommendations. In both cases, the "rebellion" had its roots in deeper conflicts between the executive and the legislature. The Nebraska legislature was caught in a tax dispute with the governor. It is reported that the legislature was generous with the agencies partly in order to embarrass the governor's opposition to a major new tax. The Wisconsin legislature, in contrast, balked at the recommendations of an unusually generous governor, and cut deeply into the requests of several agencies that he had passed intact to the legislature. (See pp. 81–82.)

Some of the conflicts between executives and legislators over the budget are bolstered by strong legislative institutions. The Budget Board of the Texas legislature is known for its independence in reviewing the governor's recommendations. It has more investigatory resources than counterparts in other state legislatures, and it has demonstrated an ability to make independent assessments of agency budget requests.

Some types of agencies are more likely than others to generate conflict between the executive and the legislature. State colleges and universities fit prominently into this role. Perhaps their large and growing budgets and the political saliency of their requests make these institutions the source of frequent disputes in state government. In most states, the higher education budget is second only to the highway budget in its demands on state government expenditures. The personal importance of higher education to many voters, and the disputes that occasionally surround campus upsets may help to make the college and university budgets especially important to some legislators.

4. Changes in regional consultation

Some observers have alleged that the practice of regional consultations is disappearing from American politics. The "nationalization" of policy is typically viewed as a fragment of larger developments that are producing an integrated national economy and culture. A number of activities are said to reflect the growing nationalism at the same time that they may further its development: the prominence of network programming on television, the absorption of locally-owned newspapers into national chains, the absorption of local industries by national corporations, the growing homogeneity of working conditions and consumer goods across the country, the development of national "labor markets" for many professions and skilled trades, and the increasing number of state and local government programs that receive funds and performance standards from federal agencies.

It is clear from our findings in Chapter VI that pressures for national uniformity have not destroyed regional routines and homogenized the policies of American states, yet the policies of certain regions are coming to resemble more and more those of the "national average." Since 1902 there has been a clear progression upward in the government spending of southern states. Governments in the Southeast spent 33 percent of the national average in 1902 and 80 percent of the national average in 1962.

It is not only in expenditures that southern governments have altered their regional norms and approached national standards of policy. The increase of state and local government spending in the South appears to be part of a larger change which is elevating public service levels more rapidly than in the country at large. Not all of the changes are home grown in the South. Much of the increase in spending may reflect state and local government responses to federal aids, which provide disproportionate incentives to the low income states in that region. Southern programs must comply with performance standards that come from Washington along with the money. In the field of race relations, integration is, at the least, a real issue in most southern communities. With the increased participation of Negroes in state and local politics, even conservative southern politicians accept the most basic demands of Negro organizations. In the state of Georgia, for example, Governor Lester Maddox has been pressed into actions that his more liberal predecessors were unable to do in their time. Partly under the pressure of federal guidelines, and partly out of respect for the increasing Negro electorate Maddox has appointed many more Negroes to middle-level jobs with the state government than did his more "moderate" predecessors Carl Sanders or Ernest Vandiver.

5. Attacks on the spending-service cliche

Although the assumption of an oversimplified spending-service relationship appears to be common among budget-makers and observers of financial decisions, the spending-service cliche is not without its critics. For many years, practitioners and commentators have tried to devise techniques that will make a rational assessment of financial needs. One recent effort has received widespread attention among economists, political scientists, and public administrators. This reform is actually a related series of devices, whose description is confused by the failure of advocates to agree on a common set of terms. Systems analysis, cost-benefit analysis, cost-effectiveness, and program budgeting have been used to describe the principal components. A common label for the entire complex is "PPBS" (Planning-Programming-Budgeting System).

PPBS seeks greater rationality in budget decisions by clarifying the cost of agency programs and the cost of alternatives to current programs. Its major components are:

1. defining the major programs of an agency
2. defining the principal "outputs" (goals) of each program
3. identifying alternative sets of 'inputs" (i.e., alternative ways of producing each major output); inputs include various combinations of personnel, facilities, and techniques of rendering service
4. computing costs of alternative combinations of inputs, and the value of the outputs likely to be produced by each combination
5. calculating the cost-benefit ratio associated with each combination of inputs and outputs

PPBS guides those who would employ public resources in the most efficient manner. If its practitioners are thorough, they should be able to identify the set of inputs that produces the lowest cost-benefit ratio of inputs to outputs.

The experience with PPBS is too current for a thorough assessment of its potential and limitations. It has been adopted in various ways by numerous government agencies, and a wide body of literature is growing out of their experience.[4] However, some shortcomings appear inherent in the system. These resemble the factors that we cited as confusing the decision-making situation, and promoting the use of the spending-service cliche (see pp. 107–113): an inability to comprehend the full range of political and economic issues associated with each major policy; and the failure of participants to abandon their familiar routines and accept policy recommendations that evolve from the new system.

PPBS actually threatens several of the routines that we have discussed in this book. By encouraging officials to examine the costs of all their programs, it discourages incrementalists from accepting the "base" of existing spending and evaluating only the increment of expenditure increase from one budget period to the next. PPBS is often described as "zero-based budgeting" in order to distinguish it from incrementalism. PPBS also discourages regional consultations among the officials of state and local governments by focusing their attention away from established programs and toward alternative projects that might obtain similar goals for less cost. PPBS is perhaps most threatening to the spending-service cliche. If adopted and taken seriously, it would mean that administrators could no longer justify increases in spending with no concern for which of the many "inputs" in a service operation actually produced their outputs. PPBS will add to the tools and to the work of budget-makers. It is possible that officials will learn to use the new tools in order to justify the increases in spending that they come to desire for reasons that are not dependent upon sophisticated benefit-cost analysis. Yet even experiments with PPBS serve to dislocate people from their established routines; such experiments often are opposed because of the "costs" of these inconveniences.

There are also problems of details in the PPBS analyses that have been made. A frequent problem lies in the choice of outputs and inputs that are selected for the analysis. Those who use PPBS tend to assess benefits and costs by looking at easily measured inputs and outputs. One budget analysis of a program to discourage high school dropouts, for example, estimated the *benefits* from the earning power of pupils who would be counseled to remain in school, and measures the *costs* of an anti-dropout program directed at high school pupils.[5] It is more difficult to quantify the social benefits accruing to a later generation of children whose parents had remained in high school until graduation (and who might have been inspired to further education). However, this benefit may be the most important contribution of an anti-dropout program to social and economic development. It is also more difficult to assess the relationship between special programs begun in the lower grades and the students' eventual completion of high school. However, it is this special program, directed at social groups that are likely to contribute a disproportionate share of the dropouts, that may offer the most efficient anti-dropout activity. In light of the complex and debatable choices that a PPBS analyst must inevitably make, it remains tempting to use the spending-service cliche, to request incremental budget increases, and to consult with regional neighbors when looking for new ideas.

Another problem of PPBS lies in its lack of concern with the "political costs" associated with alternative sets of inputs. Throughout the agencies, Department Budget Offices, Budget Bureau, House and Senate Appropriations Subcommittees, there are established loyalties, commitments and accommodations to program supporters. These obligations are linked through complex arrangements with commitments to other figures in national politics, to individual communities, and to state and local authorities. Once commitments are made, they find support in the respect for the past which is built into incremental budgeting. Professor Aaron Wildavsky is one of the most outspoken critics of PPBS. In his view, it fails to supply decision-makers with information about three aspects of political cost:[6]

1. exchange costs, i.e., the costs of calling in favors owed, or the costs of making threats in order to get others to support a policy
2. reputational costs, i.e., the loss of popularity with the electorate, the loss of esteem and effectiveness with other officials and the subsequent loss of one's ability to secure programs other than those currently under consideration
3. the costs of undesirable redistributions of power, i.e., those disadvantages that accrue from the increase in the power of individuals, organizations, or social groups who may become antagonistic to oneself.

An advantage to incremental routines is that they sharply limit the political costs which have to be calculated. When incrementalists accept the base of previous expenditures, they excuse themselves from reviewing the whole range of tradition, habits, and prior commitments that are subsumed within existing programs. PPBS threatens to perpetuate controversy (and discomfort for budget-makers) with its rationalist analysis of alternative approaches to each major program.

FACTORS THAT PROVOKE DEVIATIONS FROM ROUTINES

We do not know enough about the routines of politics to list with certainty the factors that will provoke deviations. However, we can identify certain factors that coexisted with the most apparent deviations from our routines. These are major national trauma; decisions taken at one level of government which affect routines at another level; changes in the level of economic resources within a jurisdiction; and the combination of several occurrences into a situation that is "ripe" for a change in routines. We make no claim that these categories cover the range of identifiable factors which provoke changes in routines. Indeed, the fourth category includes a number of happenings that defy a general label. It is possible that an examination of additional cases will provide more coherent structure to our assessment of deviations from routines. Because political actors are creative, however, it seems likely that the "ripe combination" of many factors will continue as an explanatory classification.

1. Major national trauma

The major national trauma associated with deviations from routines include the Depression of the 1930s and the wars of 1941–45, 1950–53, and the late 1960's. We noted above that the principal instance of change in voting allegiances occurred with the 1932 election of Franklin Roosevelt, while subsequent deviations from the Democratic majority took place in the war-impacted elections of 1946, 1952, and 1968. The standard interpretations of these elections cite voter discontent with prevailing social and economic conditions as leading many of them to depart from past allegiances.

Granting that depression and war had something to do with the deviating elections of 1932, 1946, 1952, and 1968, it is not clear that a national trauma assures that many voters will switch their loyalties. There was no major defeat for the incumbents during the congressional elections of 1950, or during the presidential election of 1944. Indeed, one slogan that was used during the 1944 campaign ("Don't Change Horses in Mid-Stream") suggests that national trauma may actually reinforce the voters' acceptance of established loyalties under certain conditions. Where the voters expect early relief from the trauma, routine loyalties may prevail. Where the crisis appears to be stalemated, or where its length has been great, the discomforts and anxieties may lead an abnormal number of voters to switch party allegiances. These same conditions may also lead many *new* voters to support a different party than their backgrounds would suggest.

The trauma of depression and war also had their impact on the routine of incremental budgeting. As in the case of stable voting patterns, however, the crisis affected deviations, but seemed not to destroy the routines. Customary patterns of incrementalism survived, and thereby testified to their appeal among budget-makers. The Depression saw the greatest incidence of deviations by state governments from typical patterns of incrementalism. There were more deviations in 1929–39 from the standard rates of expenditure change than during ten other periods between 1903 and 1965.[7] The severe economic downturn produced these deviations by undermining the value of real property and adding to citizens' need for services. Insofar as most states relied on the property tax for a major source of their revenue during the 1920s and early 1930s, devaluations meant severe losses for many state and local governments. Despite the drop in economic resources, however, federal and state government spending increased during the depression in order to meet the increased service demands. The federal government began grant-in-aid programs for old age assistance, aid to families with dependent children, aid to the blind, child welfare, the distribution of surplus agricultural commodities, wildlife restoration, soil conservation, and support for grazing lands. Twenty-three of the states adopted a tax on retail sales between 1932 and 1939; this was an effective revenue device for collecting large sums in small and unobtrusive levies. The combination of increased service needs and the differential adoption of new revenue sources contributed to the weakening of previous expenditures as the base for calculating new expenditures. Nevertheless, there is a significant coefficient of simple correlation between per capita state government expenditures in 1929 and 1939 ($r = +.43$); it testifies to the strength of incrementalism under the most trying of financial situations.

World War II, to a lesser extent the Korean Conflict, and the Viet Nam conflict to an as-yet unknown extent presented the unusual setting for domestic government agencies to *fall behind* their previous year's expenditures. During the early 1940's and 1950's, there was a sharp initial drop in the combined domestic spending of federal, state, and local governments followed by moderate increases. Much of the decrease in spending reflected the scarcity of resources brought about by the wars. Both manpower and money became less available for domestic purposes. The number of state and local government employees declined during World War II, and the magnitude of federal aids also declined.

The two periods of reconversion following World War II and the Korean Conflict saw dramatic increases in domestic spending. There were complementary increases in state and local taxes, federal aids, and state and local employees, as domestic activities were tuned-up to make up for war-time slack, and to provide for the increasing population.

The high levels of federal expenditure that were reached during World War II seemed to lessen the willingness of officials to continue with the routines of incremental budgeting and the spending-service cliche. In the executive branch, the reform movement which has now evolved to PPBS got a beginning in 1946 when the Navy Department re-organized its budget to emphasize the program components which its expenditures would purchase.[8] In 1949 the Hoover Commission urged the adoption of *performance budgeting* within federal agencies. This style of budgeting—like the earlier innovation in the Navy Department—would call the attention of budget reviewers to the levels of program output that were promised by each agency's request. This reform was initiated in the Budget and Accounting Act of 1950, and a number of federal agencies took steps to clarify the outputs that funds would purchase.

In the legislative branch, two postwar budget reforms were designed to alter the routine examination of each agency's budget request. Instead of comparing each agency's request with its own previous budget, Congressmen wanted to compare each agency's request with those of all other agencies. Their goal was the most efficient allocation of resources among alternative programs. Congress adopted the Legislative Budget in 1947 and 1948, and the Omnibus Appropriations Bill in 1950.

The major innovation of the Legislative Budget was a ceiling on total appropriations that would be voted by the House and Senate prior to deliberations by the Appropriations Subcommittees. It was expected that this ceiling would be determined after due consideration of the nation's needs, and then it would discipline the subcommittees against undue generosity. This reform was consistent with the conservative, economizing orientation of the Republican 80th Congress, and reflected the majority's sentiment that federal spending was too high. Despite the general sentiment in favor of economy, even the Republicans in control of the 80th Congress could not agree on specific remedies. During the first year of the Legislative Budget, the House and Senate did not agree on its ceiling. In the 1948 session they did agree on a ceiling, but the Appropriations Subcommittees found it impossible to remain within their allocation. The sum of their appropriations surpassed the previously-agreed-to maximum, and the Legislative Budget fell into disuse.

The Omnibus Appropriations Bill was a second effort to develop a rational-comprehensive procedure for reviewing the budget. It did away with the division of the budget among separate subcommittees. In 1950 the entire Appropriations Committee in each House sat as a body to review the budget. Presumably, this would encourage legislators to evaluate needs across departmental lines. But the reform generated more confusion than order. The job was too big for one group of Congressmen. Committee members supporting the requests of individual agencies traded votes with one another in order to advance the interests of favored agencies. When the members felt that an agency's request was too high, they slashed percentage amounts from the budgets without taking the time to specify the application of these cuts to the agencies' programs. There was too much to do in the time allotted, there was not an organizational device to encourage specialization in the budget review; the result was less budget control than when individual subcommittees concentrated on an incremental review of individual agency budgets. After one unhappy year with the Omnibus Appropriations Bill, Congress reverted to unreconstructed incremental budgeting as practiced by Appropriations Subcommittees. Incrementalism may have severe shortcomings from the rational-comprehensive point of view because it eliminates many important considerations from budget decisions. However, it does offer the undeniable attraction of simplifying complex decisions in ways that are familiar to harried legislators.

2. Intergovernmental stimuli

There have been several instances when the grants-in-aid and program requirements of the federal government have influenced the routines employed by state and local governments. The sheer level of grants coming into a state exert an influence on state government spending that is independent of incremental budgeting. The influence of federal aid is strongest in the fields of highways and natural resources, reflecting the magnitude of federal grants for those programs.[9] The requirements that come along with federal grants also have an impact on the activities of recipient agencies. Despite strong regional norms about racial integration, and although southern governments have kicked and screamed about the "guidelines" for racial integration that affect education, welfare, and hospitals, many jurisdictions have changed their policies in order to avoid court orders and the loss of federal money. There are also more subtle stimuli which federal agencies may contribute to the alteration of regional norms and related policies. The field offices of federal agencies transmit news about program innovations among the states, and may help to elevate expenditure and service levels in the less progressive states of the South and elsewhere.

Federal grants do not have a simple or direct impact on the decisions of state or local governments. In this way intergovernmental stimuli resemble national trauma: they are not powerful enough by themselves to upset routine decision processes. In the case of both types of stimulants, the results partly depend upon other factors in the decision-makers' environment. The cases of Alabama and Rhode Island welfare expenditures during 1961–65 illustrate two kinds of deviations from incremental budgeting that were stimulated by federal grants.[10] Alabama in 1961–63 and Rhode Island in 1963–65 responded to new federal grants by departing from incremental routines in welfare budgeting. The Alabama case illustrates some factors that might lead welfare budgeteers to take early advantage of a new federal program. In contrast, Rhode Island's 1961–63 period illustrates some of the elements that can deter a state temporarily from accepting a new federal opportunity.

Alabama. During 1961–63 Alabama's expenditures per capita

for public welfare increased by 31 percent. The State's welfare expenditures in 1963 were 21 percent above the level that was predicted on the basis of 1961 spending. In an immediate sense, the increase reflected Alabama's early acceptance of certain amendments to the U.S. Social Security Act. However, this early acceptance was only a recent development in a motif that has deep roots in Alabama politics.

The move that actually increased Alabama's welfare spending was the adoption (as soon as the program became available) of the federal program for vendor payments to nursing homes. Vendor payments are made directly to the vendor of services (i.e., the nursing home), rather than to clients for the purpose of meeting the costs of specified services. Prior to 1960 Alabama provided nursing home care to recipients of its old age assistance program with federal funds given the state under an arrangement that demanded more state matching funds than were to be required under the new amendments. So immediately when the new plan became available, the Alabama Department of Pensions and Security switched to the more lucrative matching formula. With the state appropriation that was freed by this transfer, the Department financed certain hospital services for its old age pensioners. The state increased its per capita welfare spending (a measure that includes federal funds received) more than the increase in the spending of state funds alone.

This account does not mention several factors of Alabama politics which help explain the ability of its budget-makers to accept the new federal program so early. Alabama is more generous to the recipients of old age assistance than to the clients of other welfare programs. This predisposition to the poor aged, long a component of the political system, helped to set up the Department for an immediate acceptance of the new federal opportunity. Like its neighboring states, Alabama does not enjoy a reputation as a generous provider of welfare assistance. The state's economy is poor and its population takes a conservative view toward welfare. Although Alabama payments under each of the public assistance programs are considerably lower than national averages, the recipients of Old Age Assistance do relatively well. The figures below show that payments to OAA recipients rank closest to the national average.

Alabama Average Benefits,
as Percentages of National Averages, 1965

Old Age Assistance	Aid to Families of Dependent Children	Aid to the Blind	Aid to the Permanently and Totally Disabled
85	33	74	54

There are numerous other signs that Alabama treats its aged poor relatively well. The name given to their program by the Legislature (Old Age Pensions) is designed to remove some of the welfare onus from recipients. In order to provide financial assurance to the program, the Legislature has earmarked portions of six state taxes to the pension fund. OAA received $16.2 million (77 percent of its total revenues) from earmarked sources during 1962–63, while no other public assistance program received more than $160 thousand from earmarked sources. Candidates for Governor generally advocate increases in old age payments, and the eligibility requirements are liberal. Although a conservative Governor Pearson enacted a law during the early 1950s to make the families of OAA recipients responsible for some of their support, Jim Folsom made this an issue in his next campaign and had the law repealed. Alabama's interest in OAA is particularly noticeable when the program is compared to AFDC. The benefits of the aged are more than twice as high—relative to national averages—as the benefits for dependent children. Moreover, the eligibility requirements appear to be far more liberal for the aged than for dependent children. Recipient rates for OAA are more than three times as high as those of AFDC when compared to national averages.

Alabama Average Recipient Rates,
as Percentages of National Averages, 1965

OAA	AFDC	AB	APTD
337	96	113	155

When it came to dropping incremental routines in order to adopt other federal offerings during the 1961–63 period, the political and/or economic characteristics of Alabama deterred major action. The State did not adopt a program to aid the dependent children of unemployed parents, and its program to provide medical assistance to persons not receiving old age assistance has not gone beyond an insignificant number of beneficiaries. Although the medical program for the aged might further Alabama's efforts to serve its needy aged, the expense of this program—if implemented on a large scale—would have required a much larger increase in state spending than did other recent innovations. In contrast to the situation that prevailed in the acceptance of funds for vendor payments to nursing homes, there was not an established state program which provided an easy exchange of federal for state money in medical assistance. Incremental budgeting in Alabama changed in the face of a federal enactment, but it was not a federal offer alone that had an impact on state officials.

Rhode Island. During 1963–65 Rhode Island illustrated another case where a state welfare department departed from incremental budget routines in response to a federal program. But during the preceding two years Rhode Island illustrated a set of conditions that delayed certain innovations beyond the time when they became available, and postponed a federally-induced deviation from incremental budgeting. Rhode Island officials considered a new program to provide medical care for aged persons not already on the welfare rolls (Medical Aid for the Aged) during 1961. But the welfare department had committed itself to several other innovations. Welfare administrators felt their capacity for change was completely absorbed by these commitments, and they perceived that the Governor wanted to hold the line on major new expenditures. By 1964, however, the welfare department felt itself capable of a major new activity, and the new Governor (John Chaffee) lent his support to the required legislation. The program of Medical Care for the Aged was large enough to increase per capita expenditures for public assistance from $24.29 to $26.94 in one year's time. Between 1963 and 1965 the state's welfare expenditures per capita increased from 117 to 143 percent of the national average.

3. Economic resources

Changes in the level of economic activity within a jurisdiction can affect decision-makers' routines by altering the resources that are available to them. With increased prosperity, sales taxes produce more revenue as citizens spend more in retail stores, income tax receipts go up as people receive more money in wages and salaries, and the revenues from property tax go up as an active economy makes itself felt on the value of real property.

We saw in our discussion of the Depression that economic trauma can have a telling impact on the routines of incremental budgeting. It is also true that milder variations in economic conditions can have an impact on public officials. Although the national economy has remained generally healthy in recent years, there are always some jurisdictions that have more abundant resources than others, and some that experience economic improvements or discomforts while the nation-wide picture appears stable.

An improvement in economic conditions may not weaken the routine of incremental budgeting as much as it alters the size of increments. One of the factors taken into account by budget-makers in planning their decisions is the anticipated level of revenues.[11] The higher the economic growth rate that is predicted, the greater are the increments to be allowed the agencies. When the expenditures of state and local governments in each state are added together, they tend to be larger in those states where economic resources are greatest. When we examine the expenditures of state governments alone, however, we find inverse relationships between economic resources and government spending.[12] Low levels of economic resources tend to have a stimulating effect on the size of increments budgeted by state governments. Why do such factors as per capita personal income, urbanization, education, and industrialization stand in inverse relationships with state government spending? Low levels of economic activity are most severe in depressing the resources of local governments. Under these conditions, state governments are relatively secure with their access to the economic resources of their larger jurisdiction, they benefit from a more generous selection of federal aids, and they have a more varied taxing network to extract revenue from available resources. Because of their more favorable revenue positions, state governments assume a larger share of state-local financial responsibilities and their increments tend to be largest under low-resource conditions.

4. Situational combinations

This fourth category of factors that lead to deviations from routines seems to be a class in itself, even though its members do not justify a more precise label. They include peculiar combinations of incidents that provoke a drastic change from routine behavior. We saw above that situational factors are important in the deviations from routines which are associated with national trauma and intergovernmental stimuli. The routines considered in this book may be so sufficiently attractive as decision rules that it requires a combination of several factors to dislodge officials from their customary procedures. In our previous discussion, the situational factors appeared to be secondary in importance to a prominent stimulus. In two cases that we shall report here, there appears to be no single most-prominent factor, but a variety of conditions that came together in order to create a situation "ripe" for major deviations from incremental budgeting. The cases at issue are deviations from nation-wide increments of spending-change during the 1957–62 period. Kentucky's spending per capita increased at a rate of 49 percent above the national average, while Massachusetts' per capita spending changed at a rate 18 percent below the national average.[13]

Massachusetts. Massachusetts' spending during 1957–62 represented a lag behind the average increment of growth and seems to reflect a long-developing economic adversity, a social characteristic that softened the demand to increase spending for education, an unaccommodating revenue system, and a protracted dispute between the legislature and several Governors. During each decade between 1920 and 1960 the economic growth of Massachusetts was below that of the nation. The State's population increased 35 percent over the 40 years and its residents' personal income increased 221 percent; comparable increases for the country were 69 and 343 percent. Our earlier findings suggest an inverse association between economic conditions and changes in state government spending. However, the Massachusetts example suggests that a long-developing economic lag may have a direct impact on the resources available for state expenditures.

The tax structure of Massachusetts helped to deter expenditure growth during 1957–62. State and local governments of Massachusetts remained dependent upon high-rate, controversial property taxes longer and to a greater extent than governments in other states. They received 57 percent of their tax revenue from this source during 1957 while state and local governments throughout the country received only 44 percent of their tax revenue from property. The burdensome nature of this tax may have reinforced the negative forces associated with slow economic growth in affecting spending during the 1957–62 period. The Massachusetts Legislature enacted a general sales tax in 1966, but only after a long struggle extending over the terms of several governors and including the 1957–62 period. For several years Governors and their spokesmen in the Legislature had claimed that the state government could not maintain desired standards of public service without a new tax. During this campaign, the Administration's economists reportedly issued conservative estimates of the revenue to be produced by existing taxes. Their low estimates might have lessened the willingness of other officials to approve budget increases.

Along with its economic and tax problems Massachusetts' extensive system of *private* education also worked against the normal rate of increase in expenditures. Public education accounted for much of the 1957–62 increase in total expenditures across the United States. In 1962, however, 24 percent of Massachusetts' elementary and secondary school pupils attended non-public schools. While expenditures for education in the 48 contiguous states increased by 83 percent between 1957 and 1962, Massachusetts' expenditures increased only 61 percent. (See pp. 94–95.)

Kentucky. A fortuitous combination of political factors came together in Kentucky during 1957–62 to permit dramatic increases in spending that were far beyond the norms associated with incrementalism. The individual factors were a liberal governor committed to improvements in public services; and an independently-inspired proposal in the legislature that provided a "natural" vehicle to obtain the needed revenue.

The home of Governor Bert Combs was in the impoverished mountain counties of eastern Kentucky. In contrast to what had been the usual pattern of fiscal conservatism in the Governor's office, Combs favored increased taxes and expenditures in order to improve services in education, highways, and other fields that promised economic development. Apparently without the governor's knowledge, some legislators proposed a veterans' bonus. This received support from some lawmakers who were reluctant to vote against veterans, but who hoped that a "fiscally responsible" Governor would veto the bill. The provision for funding the bonus was a bond issue, to be paid off by a small and temporary sales tax. Governor Combs saw the veterans' bonus as protective cover for a major new tax. He supported the bonus, but with a permanent 3 percent sales tax attached to it. Some conservative legislators had hoped for a veto, but they could not vote against a veterans bill that the Governor was supporting. They also had to accept the new tax because it was packaged with the bonus. On the basis of the revenues, Kentucky expenditures spurted upward. Each major increase was defended for its contribution to economic development. Education would provide training to meet the demands of modern industry; highways would provide the transportation necessary to economic progress; and expenditures for natural resources would permit the development of a state park system to attract out-of-state tourists and provide employment for residents of scenic mountain counties.

SUMMARY AND CONCLUSIONS

Although routines are stabilizing elements that bring equilibrium and conservatism to the political system, they do not bring rigidity. Participants deviate from their routines under the stimuli of national trauma, the directives or inducements of superior governing bodies, the magnitude of resources available in the economic system, and compelling combinations of otherwise bland conditions. Despite numerous deviations, we found no stimuli that seemed capable of destroying a routine. This finding may be a function of our search, or it may reflect the strength of routines considered in this book. Nonetheless, it suggests the attraction that routines hold out to political actors, and their importance in maintaining equilibrium among components of the political system.

The depression appears to have been the greatest challenge to political routines. It upset incremental budgeting in a number of states, and led an abnormal number of citizens to switch their party allegiance. Even then, however, the routines that we identified did not collapse altogether; they may have been followed during the Depression by a majority of relevant decision makers, albeit a lesser majority than during normal times. It appears that most of the people who voted in both 1928 and 1932 carried the same party allegiance from one election to the next; and there remained a significant relationship between the relative level of each state's expenditures in 1929 and in 1939. Among those governments that deviated from the nationwide rates of incremental change in expenditures, the deviations were not at all uniform. Individual conditions in the politics or economics of each state seemed to intervene in the depression's impact on budget-making. Moreover, the routines of stable allegiances and incremental budgeting returned in force after the decade of depression.

NOTES

1. See Samuel Lubell, *The Future of American Politics* (Garden City: Anchor Books, 1956), Chapter 4.

2. See my "Four Agencies and An Appropriations Sub-committee: A Comparative Study of Budget Strategies," *Midwest Journal of Political Science*, IX (August 1965), pp. 254–81.

3. See my *Spending in the American States* (Chicago: Rand McNally, 1968), Table III-8.

4. See David Novick, ed., *Program Budgeting: Program Analysis and the Federal Budget* (Washington: U.S. Government Printing Office, 1965); "Planning-Programming-Budgeting Symposium," *Public Administration Review*, XXVI (December, 1966); Robert Dorfman, ed., *Measuring Benefits of Government Investment* (Washington: The Brookings Institution, 1965); and "Planning-Programming-Budgeting," *Hearings Before the Subcommittee on National Security and International Operations of the Committee on Government Operations*, 90th Congress, parts 1–4 (U.S. Government Printing Office, 1968).

5. Burton A. Weisbrod, "Preventing High School Dropouts," in Dorfman, *op. cit.*, pp. 117–71.

6. Aaron Wildavsky, "The Political Economy of Efficiency: Cost-Benefit Analysis," *Public Administration Review*, XXVI (December 1966), pp. 292–310.

7. See note 3 above.

8. Jesse Burkhead, *Government Budgeting* (New York: Wiley, 1956), pp. 134 ff.

9. See my "Economic and Political Correlates of State Government Expenditures," *Midwest Journal of Political Science*, XI (May 1967), pp. 173–92, especially Table II.

10. The following reports about Alabama, Rhode Island, Massachusetts, and Kentucky are reported in more complete fashion in my *Spending in the American States, op. cit.*, Chapter VIII.

11. John P. Crecine, "A Computer Simulation Model of Municipal Resource Allocation," a paper delivered at the Meeting of the Midwest Conference of Political Science, April 1966.

12. See my *Spending in the American States, op. cit.*, Chapter IV.

13. See note 10 above.

Index